T0358481

ROUTLEDGE LIBRARY EDITIONS:
BANKING & FINANCE

BANKING AND FINANCE IN WEST GERMANY

BANKING AND FINANCE IN WEST GERMANY

HANS-HERMANN FRANCKE AND MICHAEL HUDSON

Volume 14

Routledge
Taylor & Francis Group

LONDON AND NEW YORK

First published in 1984

This edition first published in 2012
by Routledge
2 Park Square, Milton Park, Abingdon, Oxon, OX14 4RN

Simultaneously published in the USA and Canada
by Routledge
711 Third Avenue, New York, NY 10017

Routledge is an imprint of the Taylor & Francis Group, an informa business

British Library Cataloguing in Publication Data
A catalogue record for this book is available from the British Library

ISBN: 978-0-415-52086-7 (Set)
eISBN: 978-0-203-10819-2 (Set)
ISBN: 978-0-415-52858-0 (Volume 14)
eISBN: 978-0-203-11689-0 (Volume 14)

Publisher's Note
The publisher has gone to great lengths to ensure the quality of this reprint but
points out that some imperfections in the original copies may be apparent.

Disclaimer
The publisher has made every effort to trace copyright holders and would
welcome correspondence from those they have been unable to trace.

Printed and bound by CPI Group (UK) Ltd, Croydon, CR0 4YY

Banking and Finance in West Germany

HANS-HERMANN FRANCKE
and MICHAEL HUDSON

CROOM HELM
London & Sydney

© 1984 H.-H. Francke and M. Hudson
Croom Helm Ltd, Provident House, Burrell Row,
Beckenham, Kent BR3 1AT
Croom Helm Australia Pty Ltd, First Floor, 139 King Street,
Sydney, NSW 2001, Australia

British Library Cataloguing in Publication Data

Banking and finance in West Germany.
   1. Banks and banking—Germany (West)
   I. Francke, Hans-Hermann   II. Hudson,
   Michael
   332.1'0943   HG3048

   ISBN 0-7099-1277-3

Printed and bound in Great Britain

CONTENTS

7. THE FUTURE DEVELOPMENT OF THE SYSTEM

Chapter 1

AN HISTORICAL INTRODUCTION AND AN OVERVIEW OF THE
BOOK

I Introduction

From the viewpoint of the theory of financial
intermediation, the structure and degree of sophist-
ication of the banking and financial system in West
Germany should be readily explicable: as in other
advanced capitalist economies, the credit institutions in the Federal Republic serve the primary
function of transferring funds from surplus to
deficit units. Again, given the high degree of
economic development attained in the Federal
Republic, the range and complexity of its financial
intermediaries should approximate to that in other
similarly advanced economies. There might well be
specific differences between countries in the nature
of the banking and financial system with which they
are equipped, but the role of financial intermediation is common to them all. While not denying
the validity of this approach, however, the purpose
this study is precisely to focus upon the specific
features of the West Germany system.
    Two reasons may be advanced immediately for
doing so: first, the particular nature of financial
intermediation characteristic of an individual
country cannot be seen as merely due to chance, or
as embodying some abstract logic. It is capable of
providing information as to the paths which that
country's economic development has followed and the
general political and social environment within
which it has proceeded. Relatedly, but perhaps
even more basically, the present shape and "feel"
of a financial structure, the way it performs its
functions, cannot be fully understood without our
having some idea of just why it has that shape and
no other. For some purposes, any knowledge of its
development may quite permissibly be dispensed with;
but for an insight into the way it works now and the
type of institutions which embody it, some grasp of

1

the history of that development seems necessary.

Second, the way in which a particular country has sought to organise financial flows can suggest to others facing similar problems that certain types of institutions might well be implanted in them. We need only think, for example, of the influence exerted throughout Europe in the late 19th Century by the Credit Mobilier developed in France[1]; and certain features of the German system, especially the "universal banks", have exerted a similar (though lesser) attraction upon other countries up to the present day.[2]

Both reasons may therefore be advanced in justi- fication of the approach to be followed in this introductory chapter and, to a lesser extent, throughout this study. For what would be seen as the most evident feature of the German system which distinguishes it from that in other advanced economies, especially from that in Britain and (after the New Deal banking reforms[3]) the USA, has been the dominance exerted in various fields by the "universal banks", i.e. banks which provide a full range of banking services. They "take deposits and make loans, are active in the securities business (the underwriting and issue of securities, the acceptance of securities on deposit and provision of bankers' services) and sit on the supervisory boards of non-bank corporations"[4]. This appears to provide a sharp contrast with systems in which a clear separation has been enfor- ced between various types of banking, especially between commercial and investment banking. In turn, the predominance of the universal banks in Germany has been widely ascribed to the way in which and the period during which German industrialisation took place.

A somewhat less evident feature of the develop- ment of the German financial system, but one perhaps equally determinant of its present organisation, has been, however, the fact that on three occasions in the present century it has faced virtual collapse: after the inflation of 1922/23, the bank crisis of 1931, and the destruction of the Nazi regime in 1945. The problems of the system in 1931, though not some of its probable political consequences, and the role of the state in reorganising it, can to some extent be paralleled in other advanced economies at the same time, most obviously the USA. But the other experiences mark out the history of the German system as basically _sui generis_ among economically

advanced countries, and taken together they render
explicable such features of it as the importance
attributed by West Germans today to the autonomy of
the central bank.

Other, historically specific features of the
German system need only be pointed to here, since
they and their consequences will be referred to in
later chapters, e.g. the relative narrowness of the
money and capital markets that has historically
existed in Germany, and the difficulties confronted
by open market operations of the traditional type;
or, relatedly, the fact that until the early to mid-
seventies the state was absent as a net borrower of
funds from the market. In this introductory
chapter, two features of the historical development
of the system that have been referred to above will
receive primary emphasis: the development of the
universal banks and their function, and the collapse
of the overall financial system on three occasions
this century.

II The Universal Banks

The most famous thesis as to the origin of the
universal banks and their role in German economic
development is that advanced by Alexander
Gerschenkron,[5] though some of their special features
and functions had been pointed out long before
Gerschenkron published his work. Thus Jacob
Riesser in 1911 emphasised their role in providing
the capital sums required by German industrial firms
in their founding years, in the absence of either a
supply of funds forthcoming from the general public
in sufficient quantity for the purpose or a willingness on their part to accept the risk of investing
their funds in industrial undertakings. Since, in
Riesser's view, the private banks could not meet
the capital requirements of such undertakings, which
were both "new and enormous", joint-stock banks had
had to be created for the purpose. But these banks
in turn did not merely "leave enterprises to their
fate" but retained a share in them, so as to
"exercise permanent supervision over (their) management", because the banks expected the funds they had
advanced to them to be repaid from the proceeds of an
issue of stocks and bonds once the enterprise was
sufficiently well established.[6]

What Gerschenkron did, then, was not so much to
discover the role of the universal banks in German
industrialisation as to provide a theoretical

3

rationale for it.   This rationale stemmed from his
views as to the way in which European countries
embarking upon industrialisation in the late 19th
century had both developed and been forced to
develop means of financing that process which the
early starter, England, had solved in other ways.
Thus, he argued, the industrialisation of Europe
should be seen as a process that was diffused from
Britain during the 19th Century.   A country could
then be defined as "backward" by reference to the
date at which its industrialisation began, and the
greater the degree of its backwardness the greater
would be its variation from the British pattern of
growth.   Two such variations are of most importance
in the present context: first, a large scale of
industrial plant is involved, and primary emphasis
is upon the producers' goods sector rather than that
of consumers' goods;   and secondly, a much greater
role is played   "by special institutional factors
designed to increase the supply of capital to the
nascent industries and, as well, provide them with
less decentralized and better informed entrepreneurial guidance".[7]   Germany then fits into this
scheme in the following way: when Britain began to
industrialize, it did so on the basis of relatively
small-scale firms, whose growth could be financed by
reinvesting profits and required little in the way of
specialised entrepreneurial skills.   When Germany
began its industrialisation, the process had been
rendered very much more difficult by the far greater
complexity of technology and markets, and far more
capital was required if the optimum scale of plant
was to be installed.   Similarly, entrepreneurial
talent was scarce.   Hence, in a formulation which,
although applying to Europe as a whole, is seen as
fitting the German case well, "it was the pressure
of these circumstances which essentially gave rise
to the divergent development in banking over large
parts of Europe as compared to Britain.
Continental practices in the field of industrial
investment banking must be conceived of as specific
instruments of industrialisation in a backward
country".[8]
    The argument appears initially persausive,
especially since it links so closely with what
contemporary observers such as Riesser emphasised as
the main role of the universal banks.   Subsequent
criticism of it has taken two main lines, both
questioning the actual significance of such banks
for German economic development.   The first argues
that there is both a dating and a location problem

4

involved in the thesis.   Thus Cameron points out
that the "heroic age" of German industrialization
should be seen as falling roughly between 1834 and
1870, but the great majority of the large joint-
stock banks were not formed until after 1870.[9]
There is also a location problem: it was the
Rhenish private bankers who were closely involved in
the process, and who developed the type of
industrial promotional and financing activities so
firmly associated afterwards with the joint-stock
"universal banks".[10]
    The second line of criticism is a product of
the new econometric history, and questions the
efficiency of the universal banks as a system for
financing German economic development.   This
suggests that the banks inhibited rather than
stimulated German development because of the policies
they followed in their allocation of credit among the
various economic sectors.   In particular, it has
been asserted, there was a bias towards heavy
industry and against light industry, and in general
a degree of "allocative inefficiency serious enough
to have hampered the growth of non-agricultural
output" in general.[11]
    Even if both these criticisms of Gerschenkron's
thesis are correct, however, and some serious doubts
have been raised in connection with the second,[12]
they do not set aside the basic fact of a closeness
of relationship between the banks and industry which
does not really have a parallel in either Britain or
the USA.   But a more promising line of approach
would be to look at the degree of influence actually
exerted by such banks on the structual, growth and
pricing policies of the firms upon whose supervisory
boards they were so widely represented.   After all,
the possession of substantial shareholdings and/or
seats on its supervisory board does not <u>necessarily</u>
imply anything more than an ability to "influence"
which could fall very far short of control, as the
banks found to their cost when the firms with which
they were involved got into difficulties during the
depression of 1929/33.   In this connection, the
work of Böhme is important, for it shows above all
that the relationship between the universal banks
and "their" industrial customers underwent substantial changes as the process of industrialization
continued.   In particular, disputes between the
banks and their industrial clientele as to concentration and pricing policy had already flared up in
1879, and the growing scale of industrial firms,
especially in the basic heavy industries, meant that

the initiative in determining the structural and growth policy of industry tended to pass into the hands of the firms themselves. In effect, the success of the banks in promoting concentration and suppressing competition in the interests of "market peace" had led to the creation of such large industrial undertakings that from the '90s onwards the capital sums required for further expansion began to be beyond the resources of any one of the large banks to supply, and bank consortia had increasingly to be formed for the purpose.[13] Gerschenkron in fact refers to this process when he remarks that "the sheer growth of industrial enterprises enhanced the position of individual firms to the point at which they no longer needed the banks' guidance".[14]

On the other hand, the very same factor promoted concentration among the banks themselves, so that by 1912 the eight big Berlin banks (Berliner Grossbanken) controlled 51% of all commercial banks' assets. The provincial banks continued to exist in substantial numbers, partly because the Berlin banks, located as they were in the main city for the flotation of industrial and commercial securities, tended to withdraw from regular daily business and concern themselves primarily with the large securities' flotation. While, however, the provincial banks apparently maintained their independence, they became tied more and more closely to their Berlin correspondents and could easily be swallowed up by them.[15] When this is taken into account, the Berlin banks in fact controlled 83% of the total assets of all commercial banks in 1912.[16]

Finally, if Gerschenkron's thesis overstated the novelty, ubiquity and entrepreneurial role of the universal banks, it and the discussion to which it gave rise has also led to neglect of the rest of the banking system in particular by concentrating concern upon the provision of credit to large-scale industrial firms. Even before the First World War, however, a range of other financial intermediaries, especially the local savings banks and the credit cooperatives assembled and distributed funds on a scale that was considerably in excess of the joint-stock and private banks, as the following table shows. Of course, much of the credit granted by intermediaries of this type was to small borrowers, especially in the fields of agriculture and small-scale business. Yet it must be remembered that, shortly before the First World War, some 38% of the working population were still employed in the

Introduction

"primary" sector (predominantly agriculture).[17]
Similarly, 89.8% of all enterprises were socalled
"small firms" (Kleinbetriebe) employing up to 5
employees, but responsible for about one-third of
all dependent employees and for the same proportion
of the net product of the sector "industry and
crafts (Handwerk)".[18]

III The Instability of the System

There was, however, one feature of the banking
system which, at least to an observer whose experience was purely of the British system, continuously
threatened danger: the way in which its main
private institutions conducted their intermediary
role. This was most obvious in the case of the
universal banks: while the loans they granted to
large-scale industrial firms were expected to be
repaid in a relatively short time by the proceeds
of an issue of securities by the firm, or rather by
the bank on behalf of the firm, the time was of
necessity considerably longer than that for which a
British bank would normally extend credit to one of
its borrowers. Moreover, the German procedure did
appear to make the recovery of their liquidity by the
banks highly vulnerable to changes in the prevailing
sentiment on the stock market and hence to the
reception it would give to a flotation. This was
even more the case if the bank retained substantial
shareholding in the firm even after it had been
successfully floated. Given that the banks worked
with very low liquidity ratios anyway,[20] the dangers
seemed obvious, though historically they had not
really eventuated. The savings banks (and the same
could be said of the credit cooperatives) seemed
rather less prone to such liquidity problems: the
great bulk of their business remained in savings
deposits, whose volume could be expected to be
relatively stable and could therefore be converted,
with a much higher degree of security, into long-
term lending. What was to prove a source of
instability for them, but not till the depression
period of 1929/33, was their peculiar legal
position: as bodies wholly owned and controlled by
particular local government authorities, they were
open to pressure from those authorities to place
large proportions of the funds they had accumulated
from depositors into very highly illiquid obligations issued by the local authorities themselves.[21]
In both cases, however, while general economic

Table 1.1: Deposits with German Credit Institutes, 1910 and 1913[19]

(in mill. Marks)

Year	Large Berlin Banks	Provincial Banks	Total	Mortgage Banks	Savings Banks	Credit Cooper- atives
1910	4482	4241	9123	705	16781	3619
1913	5149	4493	9642	809	17882	3908

conditions remained to any degree favourable, there
seemed to be little cause to worry about the
possible consequences of their divergence from the
British model in their intermediating behaviour.

In any case, it is difficult to believe that the
particular nature of that intermediation was in any
meaningful sense responsible for the enormous
difficulties experienced by the German financial
system in the postwar inflation.[22]   Indeed, it seems
reasonable to ask whether <u>any</u> financial system could
have surmounted the catastrophic devaluation of its
assets to which that process gave rise.   For the
proximate cause of that inflation is to be traced to
the willingness of the Reichsbank to facilitate an
enormous increase in the money supply, and that
willingness in turn to factors whose origins are far
more of a political than an economic nature.

Among such underlying causes of the inflation,
two seem to have been of crucial significance: the
deficit financing of the war and its continuance in
peace-time, exacerbated by what Germans felt to be
the need to finance the costs of the passive resistance to the French occupation of the Ruhr in 1922/23;
and reparations.   The latter was clearly political
in origin; but the former as well has been traced to
the inability of the central government both during
and after the war either to impose and collect a
level of taxation that would have been necessary to
prevent the growth of government debt, or to acquire
that legitimacy in the eye of the population which
would have enabled it to fund its debt.   The
characteristic of German central government finances
after 1918 especially was an enormous and acceler-
ating rise in its floating debt, composed of central
government obligations which the Reichsbank stood
ready to discount without restriction and thus to
enable the money supply to show an enormous increase.

Moreover, as prices rose, the demand for credit
from the financial system also rose in proportion
simply to finance a volume of business stable in
real terms, as well as enable the purchase of real
assets on which speculative gains could be made.
And if such credit was not forthcoming, the result
could well have been a complete collapse of industrial activity in a country still subject to revolu-
tionary attempts to change its political constitution
and to uncertainty as to its reparation burdens and
even to the future shape of its political frontiers.
It was possible to initiate by restrictive monetary
policy a sharp business downturn in Britain and the
US in 1920/21 to come to terms with the inflationary

overhang from the war, but the fragility of German
political institutions made it unlikely that such a
sharply deflationary policy could have been followed
there.[23]

Once inflation accelerated, it became virtually
impossible for German financial institutions to
present balance sheets with any economic meaning:
the real purchasing power represented by a loan of
a given nominal amount deteriorated rapidly from day
to day, as did that represented by the interest and
amortization payments upon it.   In fact, the large
banks ceased to issue balance sheets at all in 1922
and 1923.[24]   While there was some shift to account-
ing in terms of stable currency units, especially
the dollar, the principle of "Mark equals Mark"
retained its dominance during the whole of the
period.[25]   When the mark was finally stabilized,
the financial institutions were simply permitted to
construct new balance sheets in terms of gold marks
as of 1 January 1924; even then, the figures which
appeared in them reflected simply the valuations
placed on their assets and liabilities by the firms
themselves.   As Hardach points out, "their opening
balances reflected not so much the heritage of the
past but rather an evaluation of the future earnings
of the bank".[26]   There was some writing-up of debts
to compensate for the loss of purchasing power
inflicted upon them by the inflation, especially of
government debts, but it was tardy and represented
only a very small proportion of such losses.[27]

What the inflation had done, however, was not
merely to accelerate the process of concentration in
the banking system in particular, but also to bring
about a substantial weakening in its balance sheet
position.   The figures reflecting this development
are subject to substantial difficulties of interpretation, but Lüke has estimated that the banks lost
up to 35.9% of their paid-in share capital and 31%
of their true reserves.[28]   And what was of equal
significance was that there had also occurred a
pronounced shift in the term structure of deposits
with the banks.   Thus, in the case of the large
Berlin banks, deposits of from seven days to three
months had constituted 29.8% of their total deposits
in 1913, but 40% in 1924, and deposits of more than
three months had fallen from 13.4% to only 2.5%.
Similarly for the savings banks: at the end of 1913,
savings deposits had accounted for 99.7% of their
total deposits and current accounts (Giroeinlagen)
for only 0.3%; at the end of 1924, the proportions
were 48.1% and 51.9% respectively.[29]

Introduction

This in itself would have been serious enough, given the potential liquidity dangers arising from the way in which German banking conducted its business, as has already been pointed out.   But in addition, Germany during the 1920's appeared to be suffering from a "capital scarcity", exemplified for contemporaries by the persistently large interest rate differential that persisted between Germany and other advanced economies.[30]   Faced with a persistently high level of demand for credit, in conjunction with a weakened base of own funds with which to (at least partly) meet it, the German banking system in general and the large Berlin banks in particular turned increasingly to foreign inflows of funds to fill the gap.   Thus in 1928, foreign short-term deposits in German banks made up 43.4% of their total deposits.[31]   Yet such foreign funds were not merely dominantly short-term in nature; even more, the willingness of their owners to retain them in Germany was highly vulnerable to both fluctuations in the level of economic activity in Germany and to more narrowly political factors, e.g. the unsettled position with reparations and political developments within Germany itself.

While the savings banks and credit cooperatives had not been so heavily involved in the inflow of short-term funds as the large commercial banks, the savings banks in particular were placed in a vulnerable position by their peculiar legal relationship to their sponsoring/owning local government authorities.   In effect, they were wholly under the influence of such authorities, and with the outset of the depression the ominous features of this relationship were actualized.   For the local authorities were faced with a sharp decline in their revenues from the taxation they were empowered to levy, while simultaneously they faced sharply increasing expenditures on unemployment benefits, especially since the central government sought to ease its difficulties in this field by shifting onto their shoulders an increasing proportion of its responsibility.   In this situation, they turned to "their" savings banks for finance, who were thereby put into an almost totally illiquid position.[32]

When, then, outflows of foreign funds and a domestic withdrawal of deposits began in early 1931, the latter spurred by the collapse of the textile firm Nordwolle and the large Berlin bank most closely associated with it the Darmstädter and National (Danat), the banking system necessarily entered into very great difficulties.   Nor could the Reichsbank

do much to help it: it had no power to conduct
open market operations, and its ability to provide
finance by rediscounting bills was limited by the
condition imposed upon it by international law that
it could not allow the gold and foreign currency
backing for its note issue to fall below 40%. A
bank holiday was declared on 14-15 July 1931, but
the Reich government had also to intervene to save
the threatened banks. It did so by conducting
reconstruction schemes involving complex provisions
for writing down the banks' capital and the
injection of funds by acquiring shareholdings in
them: in fact, as a result of the rescue schemes it
mounted, it ended up owning 91% of the Dresdner
Bank, 70% of the Commerzbank and 35% of the Deutsche
Bank.[33] It also introduced legislation to provide
for greater regulation of the system, and to confer
upon the savings banks a much higher degree of
independence from local authorities.[34]

What emerged from the crisis of 1931 was a
system somewhat more concentrated and somewhat more
subject to supervision. It remained one, however,
in which the dominant institutions, the large
commercial banks, were retained under private
control: by 1936, they had quietly bought back from
the government its shareholdings in them, so that
they had in effect been "reprivatized" by that date.
They were to be able to make little use of this
recovery of their full freedom of operation, though,
for they together with the rest of the financial
system were soon to be pressed into the financing of
rearmament and war.

What rearmament and war meant for the traditional clientele of the banks, industrial firms, was
a sharp rise in their profits, and hence an ability
to substantially lessen their dependence upon the
banks in particular and financial intermediaries in
general for funds with which to finance expansion.
The assets of the financial system therefore became
very largely obligations issued by the central
government, assets which were of value only so long
as that government remained in possession of
authority. Its collapse in 1945 therefore implied
the virtual devaluation of that part of the financial
system's assets; yet their liabilities, in the form
of deposits of firms and individuals with them,
remained current. Another reorganisation of the
system became necessary, and it was effected as part
of the Currency Reform in 1949. So far as banks'
liabilities were concerned, they were written down
in the ratio 100:6.5. On the assets side,

standardized norms were drawn up for the provision
of the system with own capital and liquid funds,
which were unrelated to the previous levels of these
items, and these were then effected by such means as
giving to each credit institute an initial allocation
of liquid funds at the central bank and the issue to
them of "equalisation claims" bearing a low interest
rate and regarded as debts of the new Länder.[35]

IV Conclusion and Overview of the Book

This historical survey of the German banking and
financial system has concentrated upon the two
aspects of it that may be said to constitute its
distinguishing characteristics, at least among
advanced economies: the nature and role of the
universal banks, and the instability and collapse of
the system on several occasions during this century.
Other features of that development will be touched
upon in the relevant chapters of this study.
   To the observer whose knowledge of banking
systems stems largely from the experience of the
Anglo-Saxon countries, moreover, these two features
would once have been seen as being quite closely
interconnected. Against that background, the type
of financial intermediation practiced in Germany
throughout its modern history has continually dis-
obeyed the first rule of "sound banking". Especially in the field of industrial financing, it has
appeared systematically to lead to a degree of mis-
matching of the maturities of assets and liabilities
("borrowing short and lending long") which must of
necessity lead to recurrent liquidity crises. Yet
the validity of this view must be open to doubt if
two facts are borne in mind. First, despite the
rules of "sound banking", British and US banks have
both before and even more after 1945 increasingly
involved themselves in such activities. And
second, while not changing its allegedly "unsound"
practices, the West German banking system has in
fact been virtually immune to crises since 1945.
What the system has apparently undoubtedly produced
is a degree of interlinkage between the financial
system and large-scale industry that has promoted
the elimination of competition in both spheres and
created positions of excessive market power.
   Yet, while there can be no denying the fact
of the extensive interpenetration of industry and
finance that has been historically characteristic of
Germany, the other items in the equation appear less

clear-cut.   After all, British and American
observers can find about the same degree of concentration in both the financial (e.g. the "Big 4" banks
in Britain) and industrial sectors in their own
countries, yet without the same degree of interpenetration between these sectors that apparently
exists in Germany.   Similarly, the nature of that
relationship in situations in which it does exist is
now seen as rather more problematical than used to be
the case: participation (even "substantial" participation) does not necessarily mean control.   Finally, the direction of causation has been seen as
rather more complex than was often assumed: if,
in the early stages of German industrialisation, it
was the banks who took the lead in promoting
industrial concentration, it is equally clear that
during the twentieth century growing concentration
in, industry has often stimulated and/or compelled
growing concentration in the financial sector.

There can be as little doubt of the other
characteristic of the German financial system, i.e.
its collapse and reconstruction in 1923/24, 1931/32
and 1945/49.   Yet to attribute this solely or even
dominantly to the nature of German financial intermediation seems impermissible.   No one would
attribute the 1945 collapse and reconstruction to
that cause, for what financial system however
constructed could have withstood the catastrophic
defeat and division that Germany then experienced?
For the reasons pointed out above, secondly, the
1923/24 episode hardly fits into the picture of
innate susceptibility to financial upheaval.
Clearly, the behaviour of the German banking system
during the period from (say) 1924 to 1929 comes
closest to being able to be considered within that
framework: banks could have been conducted during
that period with a much greater awareness of the new
dangers that were now involved in their traditional
behaviour.   Such awareness may well have avoided
some of the willingness to indulge in the more
speculative type of business for which the Danat
was to become notorious;   but German bankers were
not alone in holding what were to prove excessively
optimistic views as to future economic developments.
After all, even supposedly soundly-run British banks
were to find large amounts of their liquidity
immobilized in ailing companies to which they had
granted credit.

The main enduring lesson that Germans have drawn
from the historical developments has not called into
question the role of the universal banks and their

efficiency in promoting economic development.   Nor
has it been merely to place immense importance upon
establishing and maintaining the autonomy of the
central bank.   Rather, given that such an autonomous central bank has been created, equipped with
the range of instruments with which it can fulfill
its primary function of safeguarding the purchasing
power of the currency, the fear has sometimes been
expressed that the creation of so powerful a central
bank is incompatible with the democratic control of
economic policy.   Thus, at times during the term of
office of the recent SDP/FDP government, it seemed
to some observers as if fiscal and monetary policy
were pulling in different directions.

The Bundesbank's apparent success in fulfilling
its main aim is indicated by the very low inflation
rates to which the West German economy has been
subject throughout most of its history, though it
might be argued that any central bank could have done
as well if it were surrounded by an environment in
which, for ample historical reasons, inflation is
feared to an extent which is probably unique among
economies at the same stage of economic development
as West Germany.   In Chapter 2 of this work, the
association in the public mind of this success with
the very substantial degree of autonomy conferred
upon the Bundesbank by its founding statute, an
autonomy for which on occasion the Bundesbank
president of the time has felt it necessary to
involve himself in public controversy with the
Federal government, is emphasised.   That chapter
deals as well with the organisation and functions of
the Bank, especially its role as the "foreign
currency bank" of the Federal Republic.   It is in
this connection that some stress is laid upon the
peculiar difficulties which the Bank has faced for
much of the period in conducting its domestic
monetary policy: the dominant role played by the
foreign component of the money supply, as compared
to that originating in borrowing by the state and
the private banking system from the central bank.
Partly this has been due to the relatively large
share of foreign trade in West Germany's Gross
National Product and the fact that its balance of
payments has been in surplus for much the greatest
part of the period since the early 1950's.   But
two other factors have also been contributory in this
respect: that the overall government sector was in
surplus, and sometimes largely so, until the early
70's;   and that the state was even otherwise debarred
by law from borrowing from the Bank.

Introduction

The most striking feature of the overall banking system operating under the control of the
Bundesbank is not so much the strength of the "Big
Three" universal banks (Dresdner, Deutsche and
Commerzbank), but, first of all, the fact that they
form only one element of a tripartite system in which
all three elements are roughly of equal strength and
between which competition is normally fierce: the
commercial banks, the public savings banks with their
regional central institutions, and the credit
cooperatives. Historically originating in special-
isation upon particular types of banking activity,
the individual elements of the tripartite system
have developed into other fields of financial
operations to an extent that makes it clear that
none of the three can take for granted that there
is any sphere in which their position is necessarily
free from attack by the others. The tripartite
system and the main types of business with which each
of its components are involved are analysed in
Chapter 3, and some attention paid there to recent
developments, especially the development of the
central giro institutions of the savings banks into
large universal banks in their own right. This
chapter also deals with other credit institutions
with specialized functions, either operating in
particular areas such as private and public construction activity or in the performance of certain
specialized public tasks such as the financing of
development aid and the reorganisation of agriculture.
Chapter 4 concentrates upon the financial
markets in the Federal Republic, with emphasis upon
two particular features of those markets: the
relative underdevelopment of the market in corporate
issues, and the fact that the household sector has
shown a marked preference for holding its monetary
assets predominantly in the form of bank deposits.
Initially at least, these features stem primarily
from the monetary reconstruction of 1948, but the
dominant role played by the credit institutions in
assembling and channelling the flow of funds
throughout the economy has only intensified since
then. Again, while the market in stocks and shares
has continued to remain relatively limited, the
state has now begun to appear in the market as a
significant borrower, with a subsequent widening in
the volume of issue of and transactions in its
securities. By comparison with the US and Britain,
business firms rely to a much higher extent upon
borrowed funds rather than those acquired by the
issue of risk-bearing equity, which has two

important consequences: first, the existence of
close links between credit institutes and firms in
the Federal Republic, and second the particular
sensitivity to interest-rate changes.

The short-term ("money market") financial
markets are similar in their dealings to the Federal
Funds market in the US and the traditional money
market in Britain, and it is in them that the
Bundesbank concentrates its monetary policy operations. Until 1973 and 1979 respectively, it did
not have the power to undertake sale and repurchase
agreements with the credit institutes but relied
instead upon influencing their liquidity by changing
its "leading rates", the discount and Lombard rates.
Chapter 5 explains in detail the nature of the
Bank's operations in this market, emphasising the
conditions upon which and the interest rate at which
the credit institutes will choose or be forced to
replenish their liquidity by borrowing from the
central bank. In this context, the elaborate
system of minimum reserve ratios applying to the
credit institutes, and the use of them made by the
Bank, is also outlined. The enlargement of the
range of instruments available to the Bank in this
market, especially with respect to foreign transactions, is then described.

In conducting its monetary policy, the Bundesbank was an early participant among central banks in
moving to the explicit adoption of a monetary target.
It did so, in fact, as soon as the floating of the
DM in 1973 relieved it of the almost Sisyphean task
it had faced until then in attempting to
"neutralize" so far as possible the massive inflows
of the funds that had been characteristic of the
'50s and 60s. As shown in Chapter 6, however, the
target it adopted was of a construction peculiar to
itself, i.e. the supply of "central bank money",
equal to coins and notes in circulation plus minimum
reserves held by the credit institutes on their
domestic obligations at the reserve ratio in force
in January 1974. The particular construction of
this aggregate was the object of much criticism
from West German economists, on the grounds of
whether it could actually be "controlled" by the
Bank, what it included and excluded from among the
relevant monetary aggregates, and what fulfillment
of it in practice actually implied for the monetary
policy being conducted. On the other hand, there
is much evidence that, to an extent similar to that
of (say) the Bank of England, the Bundesbank was
unwilling to adopt a type of target which could

create difficulties for what it felt to be its
retention of the flexibility requisite for the overall operations of a central bank.   With West
Germany's accession to the European Monetary System
in 1979, moreover, and the insertion of targets for
international interest-rate differentials and the
exchange rate of the DM into that for central bank
money, the precise extent of the Bank's adherence to
a monetary target has become even more problematic.

Finally, in Chapter 7, an attempt is made to
chart the changing contours of the West German
banking and financial system under the same
pressures of internationalization and increasing
fluidity of boundaries between the various types of
banking business that has become characteristic of
all advanced capitalist economies since the 1970s.
On the one hand, the West German credit institutions
show the same process of diffusion into new types of
activity that marks their counterparts in Britain
and the US.   Thus, savings banks, through their
central giro institutions and even in some cases by
themselves, have developed into large-scale universal
banks;   and the peculiarities of financial structure
between the components of the system are being
smoothed out either by actual processes or by
assimilation to each other of the conditions under
which the various credit institutions practice their
asset and liability management, through changes in
the law applicable to them.   If the West German
system is therefore, under the pressure of circumstances, becoming more "normal" in its structure and
operations, i.e. more like that in Britain and the
US, there is a widespread belief that it should
actually be made even more so by legal enactment.
For it is that very feature of the West German
system that has often been held to provide its
differentia specifica, the particular role of the
universal banks vis-a-vis industry, which has
increasingly come under fire.   The proposals of
various Banking Commissions for steps to be taken
to reduce the hitherto close relation between the
banking system and business firms stand little chance
of being adopted;   that they are made at all, and
emenate from such respectable quarters, is significant enough in itself.   For it suggests that there
exists in West Germany a significant body of opinion
that feels the undoubted advantages of the universal
bank in its specific German form may be linked with
less palatable features, such as its effect upon
competition in the economy and the possible increase
in the vulnerability of the banks to the effects of

a decline in the performance of the firms with which
they are so closely associated.

NOTES

1.   David Landes, The Unbound Prometheus,
Cambridge, 1969, p. 207
2.   For Britain, see the Report of the
Committee on Finance and Industry (Macmillan
Committee) (1931, Cmd. 3897), par. 384.   In a later
British appraisal, the universal banking system is
said to have played "almost (the role) of a corporate fairy godmother ... which has been of such great
advantage to the country".   Financial Times,
"Financial Times Survey : West Germany", Oct. 18,
1976, p. 20
3.   On these reforms, see e.g. Harold
Underwood Faulkner, American Economic History (5th
ed.), New York 1943, p. 659-660
4.   Wolfram Eckstein, "The Role of the Banks
in Corporate Concentration in West Germany",
Zeitschrift fur die gesamte Staatswissenschaft, 136,
3 (Sept. 1980), p. 465
5.   Alexander Gerschenkron, Economic Backwardness in Historical Perspective, Cambridge, Mass.,
1962
6.   Jacob Riesser, The German Great Banks and
Their Concentration in connection with the Economic
Development of Germany, Washington 1911, pp. 465,
343
7.   Cited in Rondo Cameron (ed.), Banking and
Economic Development.   Some Lessons of History,
London 1972, pp. 9-11
8.   Gerschenkron, op. cit., p. 14
9.   Cameron, Banking and Economic Development
..., p. 13
10.   Richard Tilly, "Germany 1815-1870", in:
Rondo Cameron (ed.), Banking in the Early Stages of
Industrialisation.   A Study in Comparative History,
London 1967, pp. 160-161
11.   Hugh Neuberger and Houston H. Stokes,
"German Banks and German Growth, 1883-1913 : An
Empirical View", Journal of Economic History, 34
(Sept. 1974), pp. 729-730
12.   Rainer Fremdling and Richard Tilly,
"Germany Banks, German Growth and Econometric
History", Journal of Economic History, 36, 2 (June
1976)
13.   Helmut Böhme, "Bankenkonzentration und
Schwerindustrie 1873-1896", in: Hans-Ulrich Wehler
(ed.), Sozialgeschichte Heute.   Festschrift fur

Hans Rosenberg zum 70 Geburtstag, Gottingen 1974
     14. Gerschenkron, op. cit., p. 139
     15. Böhme, loc. cit., p. 444.   Riesser, in the
work cited in note 6 above, shows e.g. the Deutsche
Bank, one of the large Berlin banks, as having at
least one member on the supervisory board of another
sixteen, provincial, banks.
     16. Gerd Hardach, "Banking and Industry in
Germany in the Interwar Period 1919-1939", mimeo.,
Banco di Roma, n.d., p.3
     17. F.W. Henning, Die Industrialisierung in
Deutschland 1800 bis 1914, Paderborn 1979, Table 1,
p. 20.
     18. Karl Heinrich Kaufhold, "Das Handwerk
zwischen Anpassung und Verdrängung", in: Hans Pohl
(ed.), Sozialgeschichtliche Probleme in der Zeit der
Hochindustrialisierung (1870-1914), Paderborn 1979,
pp. 109, 121
     19. Carl-Ludwig Holtfrerich, Die Deutsche
Inflation 1914-1923.   Ursachen und Folgen in
Internationaler Perspektive, Berlin 1980, Table 10,
pp. 48-49
     20. Ibid., p. 54
     21. Karl Erich Born, Die Deutsche Bankenkrise
1931.   Finanzen und Politik, Munich 1967, p. 28
     22. For a thorough study of the causes and
consequences of the inflation, see the work by
Holtfrerich referred to in note 19 above.
     23. Karl Hardach, The Political Economy of
Germany in the Twentieth Century, London 1980, p. 16
     24. Manfred Pohl, "Die Situation der Banken in
der Inflationszeit", in: Otto Büsch and Gerald D.
Feldman (eds.), Historische Prozesse der deutschen
Inflation 1914 bis 1924, Berlin 1978
     25. Otto Pfleiderer, "Das Prinzip 'Mark = Mark'
in der Inflationszeit", in: Büsch and Feldman (eds.),
op. cit.
     26. Gerd Hardach, loc. cit., p. 7
     27. Otto Pfleiderer, "Two Types of Inflation,
Two Types of Currency Reform", Zeitschrift für die
gesamte Staatswissenschaft, 135, 3 (Sept. 1979),
p. 358
     28. Rolf E. Lüke, "Die Deutsche Bankenwirtschaft
unter dem Dawes-Plan", in: Karl-Erich Born (ed.),
Moderne deutsche Wirtschaftsgeschichte, Berlin 1966,
p. 376
     29. Ibid., p. 375
     30. Gerd Hardach, loc. cit., pp. 9-10
     31. Heinrich Irmler, "Bankenkrise und Vollbes-
chaftigungspolitik (1931-1936)", in: Deutsche
Bundesbank (ed.), Währung und Wirtschaft in

Deutschland 1876-1975 Frankfurt a.M. 1976, p. 286
    32. See note 21 above
    33. Born, Bankenkrise 1931..., p. 147
    34. Ibid., p. 164
    35. Otto Pfleiderer, "Two Types of Inflation...",
pp. 362-363

Chapter 2

THE DEUTSCHE BUNDESBANK

The central bank in the Federal Republic of Germany is the Deutsche Bundesbank, founded on 26 July 1957 with its head office in Frankfurt. To an extent that certainly distinguishes the Federal Republic from most other Western industrial nations, the Bundesbank exerts a profound influence upon the monetary and financial system of the German economy and above all on monetary and financial policy in the Federal Republic. There are two reasons for the particular significance that the Bundesbank has assumed. The first is the relatively high degree of autonomy it possesses vis-a-vis the government and the private economy, which has made an essential contribution to the achievement of a domestic rate of inflation that is low by international standards. The second is a result of a rapid, externally - orientated growth of the German economy after the Second World War, a growth that would have been inconceivable without the existence of an efficient central bank whose activity was heavily influenced by the development of the international monetary· system. If these two features of the Bundesbank and its policies are to be fully understood, it is first of all necessary to briefly outline the history of its origins before its functions and organisation are discussed in detail.

I The History of the Reichsbank

If the historical development of the German central bank is compared to that of other central banks such as the Bank of England and the Banque de France, but also the US Federal Reserve System,[1] two important differences stand out: discontinuity and repeated basic reorganisation. They can be traced

22

back to the special features of Germany's historical development, i.e. the relatively late foundation of the unified Germany and two lost world wars. While these rendered impossible a continuous development of the central banking system, they nevertheless at the same time repeatedly opened up the possibility of adjusting that system efficiently by means of a rational reorganisation.

The first central bank having jurisdiction over the whole of Germany was the Reichsbank, founded in 1875 by the transfer of the Prussian Bank to the German Reich created in 1871.[2]   Given the leading role played by Prussia in the Reich, the Prussian Bank was likely to figure as the Reichsbank's forerunner, but in addition it was by far the most important of the numerous - mostly private - note-issuing banks in the various German states.[3] However, the setting-up of the Reichsbank had to face considerable opposition, because the other note-issuing banks sought to maintain their "well-established rights".   What finally convinced the opponents of the proposed Reichsbank was only the example of other countries, especially England, which had shown the economic significance and superiority of a single note-issuing authority.[4]

While the original capital of the Reichsbank was subscribed by private shareholders, the Bank itself was "under the supervision and management of the Reich".   The supervision was exercised by a Board of Trustees consisting of the Reich Chancellor and four other members;   the Chancellor, and under him a Reichsbank Board of Directors, likewise conducted the management of the Bank.   The Board of Directors in turn was headed by a President appointed for life by the Emperor on the proposal of the Bundesrat.   The Board, finally, was responsible for the actual administration and operating policy of the Bank, even though it was formally obliged "to comply in all matters with the instructions given to it by the Chancellor".

In law, therefore, the Reichsbank was largely dependent upon the government, but until the First World War it actually was able to operate with a very high degree of independence from it.   Its autonomy in practice was due for one thing to the fact that the Reich government made no use of the powers of direction available to it.   In addition, the fact that the members of the Board of Directors were appointed for life infused their decisions with a certain self-conscious independence.   Finally - and certainly, decisively - the factual autonomy of

the Reichsbank corresponded completely to the spirit
of economic liberalism dominant in the period in
which German industry was created, a period more than
fifty years later in time than the corresponding
epoch in England.   Operating wholly in line with the
precepts of the international gold standard, the
Reichsbank restricted its activities to the control
of the note issue and the management of national and
international payments, in order to maintain the gold
parity of the currency established by the state.[5]
The notes it issued were not even legal tender until
1 June 1909, and to that extent they were in law
competitive with other means of payment, especially
gold.   The monetary decisions of the Reichsbank
were therefore determined above all by influences
eminating from foreign trade, which was characterised
in the monetary sphere by the gold standard and the
dominance of London as a banking centre and of the
Bank of England.   No role at all was played in such
decisions by domestic economic considerations, _e.g._
the level of employment and the financing of the
state.[6]
     It was with the beginning of the First World
War that the Reichsbank's character changed from that
of a currency central authority of a private-law
nature, operating _de facto_ with a high degree of
autonomy from government.   By the Laws on War
Finance of 4 August 1914, it was converted into an
instrument to finance the war.   To that end, it was
freed from its obligation to redeem its notes in gold
and from the provision that it should maintain a cash
cover (consisting of gold above all, but also
including saleable German and foreign coins and the
notes of other German banks) of one-third of its
notes in circulation.   The latter provision was
altered to permit the socalled state loan fund notes
to be counted towards the cash cover.   Although the
state thereby was granted the possibility of
creating money to whatever extent it wished, the
First World War was in fact financed - in any case
until the signs of German defeat began to show themselves clearly in 1917 - relatively responsibly by
the issue of loans taken up by the private sector.
Between 1914 and the end of 1918, the volume of
circulating media in the German Reich (Reichsbank
notes, Reich deposit certificates, loan fund notes,
private bank notes and coinage) rose from 7.2 Mrd.
Mark to 29.4 Mrd. Mark.[7]
     This burden originating from the war would not
have in itself raised any serious problems for the
maintenance of the German monetary system had not the

demands placed upon the financial capabilities of the state, especially by the internal political instability and the reparations imposed by the victorious powers, proved considerably beyond its capacity to meet. When the war was over, the Reichsbank was not restored to its prewar position as an autonomous decision-making authority; rather, it was increasingly subordinated to the financial needs of the state. It thus became nothing more than the source of credit for an over-indebted German Reich, operating in accordance with the instructions given to it by the Reich Chancellor.[8] The Great Inflation of 1923 thus became inevitable, even though in 1922 the Reichsbank's autonomy had been formally restored under pressure from the victorious powers at the Cannes Conference. In fact, the subordination of the officiating Board of Directors to the Reich government remained intact. In the course of the year 1923, the monetary catastrophe came about: in September of that year, the volume of Reichsbank notes in circulation amounted to 43.595 Mrd. Mark, and in November the Reich government's debt to the Reichsbank was about 190 trillion mark.[9]

But the Bank's role underwent a basic reorientation as a result of the Bank Act of 30 August 1924 promulgated in connection with the Dawes Plan, for at the demand of the victorious powers it now obtained a complete formal independence from the government. The management of the Bank lay solely with its Board of Directors which had merely to inform the government as to the activities it was undertaking if the government requested it to do so. Simultaneously a degree of foreign control was imposed upon it by the creation of the socalled General Council and the post of Commissioner for the Note Issue.[10] Its lending to the Reich was subjected to narrow limits, and a minimum cash cover for the note circulation was prescribed: 30% in gold and 10% in foreign exchange. Hjalmar Schacht was appointed as the new Reichsbank president.[11]

During the following years of the Weimar Republic, when the Reichsbank was stabilized, there were repeated and violent disagreements between the autonomous Bank and the Reich government, dependent as the latter was upon financial assistance. Yet the Bank was able to assert itself against the government to such an extent that it can be said to have exerted considerable pressure upon the government. The culmination of this conflict came in the years 1929/30, when the government could no

longer meet its financial obligations.   Schacht
would only agree to its raising a loan from the
American banking firm of Dillon, Reed & Co. on
condition that an Immediate Programme was adopted
involving extensive budgetary cuts, rises in taxation and redemption of the Reich debt.   Schacht
was able to force acceptance of his demands and
Hilferding, the Minister of Finance, had to resign.
Yet in March 1930 Schacht himself was compelled to
resign from his post, and a reduction in the Bank's
autonomy was simultaneously effected by an increase
in the influence which the Reich President could
exercise in the appointment and recall of its
president.
      The reduction in its independence was then
systematically pushed forward from 1933 onwards
under the Nazi regime, although Schacht himself
returned to the presidency of the Bank between 1933
and 1939.   In 1937, the Bank's independence was
formally abolished, and the Board of Directors subordinated to the direction of the Führer and
Chancellor Adolf Hitler.   Finally, in 1939 a new
Reichsbank Act removed the former provisions relating to cash backing for the note issue and once again
enlisted the Bank into the service of war financing.
The wage and price controls decreed in the same year,
together with the increasing scarcity of consumer
goods and monetary expansion, resulted in a
suppressed inflation.[12]

II The Origins and Development of the Bundesbank

After Germany's unconditional capitulation in 1945,
the division of the Reich into four zones of
occupation took place as envisaged in the
Agreement of the victorious allies.   Certainly, the
Reichsbank continued to exist in a formal sense; yet
in fact it was replaced by the foundation of Land
central banks in each of the occupation zones, which
at first continued to regulate the circulation of
the old Reichsbank notes.   The Allies themselves
had no agreed-upon concept as to how the German
currency system should be reorganised;   on the
contrary, their views on this matter underwent
repeated change, and differed even among the Western
occupation powers.[13]   This was true above all of
American views, which altered, under the influence
of the deterioration of relations with the USSR,
from the rigorous policy of destruction embodied in
the Morgenthau Plan to the constructive new

beginning represented by the Marshall Plan.   A
decisive role in this development was also played by
the American military,[14] especially General Lucius
D. Clay, who were anxious to return economic responsibility into German hands as quickly as possible.
This implied serious conflicts with the Soviet Union
and at the beginning France as well, although the
latter changed its attitude in 1947 after the
detachment of the Saar.

The American concept as to the reorganization
of the German banking system took on concrete form
in several plans drawn up by Joseph M. Dodge, the
head of the financial section of the American
military government.   In adherence still to the
Potsdam Agreement, the banks together with the
central bank newly to be created were to be decentr-
alised, which implied in particular the closing-down
of the Reichsbank and the head offices of the big
banks.   In addition, the system of universal banking
was to be abolished, in order to eliminate the great
influence exerted by the banks upon German industry
and to prevent it from being restored in the future.
Both objectives were rejected by the British
government: on the one hand, they feared that a new
system along such lines would be less efficient, and
on the other the control of.the German economy would
thereby be made more difficult.   Thus, while Land
central banks after the pattern of the member banks
of the Federal Reserve System had already been
erected by 1947 in the American and French occupation zones, it was only in 1948 that a similar step
was taken in the British zone.   With a considerable
contribution and much advice from German experts,
the "Bank deutscher Länder" was then set up on
1 March 1948, with the task of coordinating the
operating policies of the individual Landeszentral-
banken (State central banks).[15]   The five Länder of
the Soviet zone did not adhere to this system;
instead, a centralised organization after the Soviet
model was set up there, headed after the currency
reform by the "Deutsche Notenbank" located in
Berlin-Potsdam.

The setting-up of the Land central banks
suggests that the American (and French) aim of
decentralization of the system was realized, but it
must be pointed out that some of the elements
essential for the later development of the German
banking system were substantially influenced by the
British view that a centralized central bank and the
universal type of bank should be maintained.
Certainly, the Bank deutscher Länder was initially

merely the central organization of the Landeszentral-
banken, but already at the time of its foundation
the task of forming the later Deutsche Bundesbank
was established.   The latter was then to obtain
significantly greater central authority and to that
extent lay wholly in the tradition of the
Reichsbank.[16]   At the same time the Bank Deutscher
Länder and especially its successor the Bundesbank
was equipped with a modern armoury of monetary and
credit instruments patterned on those possessed by
the Federal Reserve System.   But the decisive
factor was that from its beginning the Bank
deutscher Länder enjoyed a degree of independence
from government similar to that of the Reichsbank
during the Weimar Republic.   One thing that contributed to this was its federal structure, even though
it was the respective state governments which
appointed the members of the Central Bank Council,
the body which, together with the Directorate,
determined the policy of the Bank.[17]   For if any
change in the political relations within the Central
Bank Council were to take place, it could occur only
if the same political changes happened in all the
states.   Hence the Bank deutscher Länder was a
central bank possessed of a high degree of independence, which its first president Wilhelm Vocke
consistently took advantage of.[18]   Its autonomy and
the behaviour of its leading management personnel
then also stamped themselves upon the later development of the Bundesbank founded in 1956.

III The Autonomy of the Deutsche Bundesbank

The question of autonomy is undoubtedly of decisive
importance for a central bank to function efficiently.
Hence it is not suprising that disputes as to the
degree of autonomy to be afforded the Deutsche
Bundesbank delayed its foundation until 1956,
although the law relating to a Bundesbank that was
provided for in Article 88 of the Basic Law should
have been submitted by that date.   There were
proposals emenating from Parliament which aimed at
a central state bank more closely subject to
government directives in its operation; but the
scheme that was eventually adopted, while emphasising the independence of the bank and federal aspects
of it, simultaneously strengthened the central
position to be filled by its executive.   Of
decisive significance in securing this scheme were
the especially negative experiences that had been

made with a politically depdent central bank, as
well as the possibility opened up by history of
creating a newly-constructed body that would be both
rational in its organisation and relatively free
from political influences. The bank that resulted
was then an efficient mixture of centralisation in
the tradition of the Reichsbank and decentralisation
after the model of the American Federal Reserve
System.

What was by international standards a relatively high degree of autonomy of the Bundesbank was
given concrete form in all of the three presuppositions essential for independence in central
bank policy: its institutionally laid-down
structure of organisation and decision-making; the
efficiency of the monetary policy instruments with
which it was furnished (a separate chapter is
devoted to this); and the ability of its leading
personnel to ensure that it was their views and
decisions that dominated the operation of the Bank.
The first two of these presuppositions are certainly
necessary if the policy of the central bank is to be
conducted independently; but the third is also
essential, because it establishes the degree to
which the possibilities existing are actually utili-
zed.

The Deutsche Bundesbank is a juristic person of
public law directly owned by the Federal Government.
Yet, while it is the Federal Government that owns
its original capital of 290 Mill. DM and to whom
flows any profit made by it, that does not give the
government any further rights to influence the way
in which it conducts its business. Its independence is explicitly confirmed in section 12 of the
Bundesbank Law, even though, "while maintaining its
functions, it has the duty of supporting the general
economic policy of the Federal Government". What
must be emphasised is that the obligation expressed
in the latter half of the sentence quoted does not
set aside the task referred to in the first half,
and this refers above all to its function (according
to sec. 3 of BBankG) of "safeguarding the currency",
i.e. maintaining the value of money. To that
extent, the combatting of inflation forms the
central task of the Bundesbank, and in perceiving
and acting upon it the Bank is autonomous. Moreover, it takes precedence for the Bank over other
possible goals.[19]

In a way similar to that in which the judiciary
is independent of the government, the stabilization
of the value of money has therefore been assigned

to an independent institution which thereby
exercises a sort of "fourth power", despite the fact
that its ability to do so is not laid down in the
constitution of the Federal Republic. The special
legal position of the Bundesbank could only be
changed by parliament (the Deutsche Bundestag)
deciding to amend the Bundesbank Act. For the rest,
the control which can be exercised over the
Bundesbank by parliament and the government is
restricted to ascertaining whether it has acted within its legal competence. Of course, a fundamental
possibility open to parliament is the setting-up of
committees to serve in the preparation of important
laws relating to monetary policy or to investigate
new developments in central banking. In fact,
however, no investigative committees have hitherto
ever been appointed in the Federal Republic which,
like the British Select Committees on the National-
ized Industries or the Committees of Congress in the
U.S., would undertake a comprehensive examination
of the policy followed by the central bank.20

By comparison with this legal position of a
high degree of autonomy, the Bank of England is
subject to an essentially greater extent to
direction by the government and supervision by
parliament, for its nationalisation was one of the
first steps undertaken by the Labour Party when it
come into office after the Second World War.
Previously a privately-owned institution, the
British central bank was thereby transformed into a
state establishment subject to directive by the
Chancellor of the Exchequer, even though scarcely
any use has been made of this power. Hence the
legal position of the central banks in the Federal
Republic and Britain (as in France as well) has
tended in recent times to develop in precisely
opposed directions. While in the former a
Bundesbank independent of government control has
been developed from the dependent Reichsbank of the
Nazi period, in the latter a state central bank
formally subject to the instructions of the
government has replaced the private and largely
independent Bank of England.

Yet even in the Federal Republic the government
does possess some influence upon the personal composition of the Bank's most important decision-making
body, the Central Bank Council (Zentralbankrat), via
its voice in the selection of that body's members.
Nevertheless, this influence - as also obtained in
the case of the Bank Deutscher Länder - is so
greatly limited by the federal element in the

Council's composition that it can have virtually no
effect upon the current operations of the Bank.   In
addition to the members of the Board of Directors
(President, Vice-President, and up to 8 other
directors, although there are currently only four of
the latter), the Central Bank Council is composed of
the presidents of the eleven Land central banks.
The president, vice-president and other directors
are appointed for a term of eight years by the
Federal President upon their nomination by the
Federal government, with the Council having the right
to express its views in this matter;   during their
term of office, these members cannot be dismissed.
The presidents of the Land central banks are appointed on the nomination of their respective Land
governments.   Given that in general different
political parties are in office in the Federal
government and in the Länder, and also that parlia-
mentary elections take place at different times at
the various levels of government, the Federal government is in fact unable to exert any sudden influence
upon the composition of the Council to create a
majority for a particular policy orientation.
The following diagram illustrates the composition of
the Council:21

THE CENTRAL BANK
COUNCIL OF THE
DEUTCHE BUNDESBANK

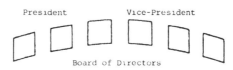

President   Vice-President

Board of Directors

Appointed by the Federal President on the
nomination of the Federal Government

Appointment of the Presidents of the Land Central Banks
by the Federal President on the nomination of the
Federal Upper House (Bundesrat)

Presidents of the Land Central Banks

As a general rule, the Council meets every two
weeks and arrives at its decisions by simple
majority.   Members of the Federal government can
participate in the Council's Meetings and put forward
resolutions, but they have no vote.   The Council
determines the Bank's monetary and credit policy and
lays down guiding-lines for its conduct of business
and its administration; in particular cases it can
also give instructions to the administration.   Its
decisions are carried out either by the Bank itself
and/or by the Land central banks, which form the
chief administrative offices of the Bank in the
individual Länder.   In contrast to the extremely
federalist two-stage constitution of the Bank
deutscher Länder, which was separate from the legally
independent Land central banks, the Bundesbank Law
therefore effected a centralisation of the German
central banking system along the lines of the previous structure of the Reichsbank.   The Land central
banks certainly conduct any business of purely
regional significance on their own responsibility,
but as chief administrative offices of the Bank they
are subject to its directives.   They are also
equipped with boards composed of representatives of
the credit institutions, the economy and labour, who
advise the bank's board of management.   They maintain branch offices (currently numbering about 200)
in the larger towns (the socalled "places where there
is a Bundesbank office"): the dominant task of such
offices is to provide the economy with central bank
money and to transact payments by draft etc.
The decision-making and organisational structure
of the Bundesbank depicted above shows considerable
similarities to that of the US Federal Reserve System.
Thus the Central Bank Council is comparable to the
Board of Governors, and the eleven Land central banks
correspond to the twelve Federal Reserve Banks.   Yet
important differences between the structure of the
two central banks also exist.   Thus, the Federal
Reserve Banks possess greater independence vis-a-vis
the Board than do the Land central banks in relation
to the Central Bank Council.   The reason is that
the Federal Reserve Banks are actually owned by their
member banks, whose representatives on the board of
directors outnumber those named by the Board.[22]
Again, the members of the Board are appointed by the
President of the United States for a term of office
of 14 years which runs beyond the period for which
the government is elected.   Yet up to the present,
every Governor of the System whose policy was not in
line with that of the Executive has resigned his post.

To that extent, basic conflicts between the government and the Federal Reserve System tend to be more short-term in nature and a change in course in American economic policy following upon a change of government can generally be assumed to bring with it a certain corresponding adjustment of the policy followed by the Board of Governors, although there is no necessary reason de jure why this should occur.

In the Federal Republic, on the contrary, there have been repeated conflicts between Bundesbank and government, and while they have not been fought out in public they have nevertheless been of considerable significance for the tendency of economic policy. Their basic source is to be found in the difficulty of reconciling a policy aimed at stabilising the purchasing power of money with one more orientated towards the level of employment and economic growth. They take on concrete shape whenever the government - normally in periods of recession - becomes concerned to stimulate employment and growth while the Bundesbank, in accordance with the task imposed upon it by law, seeks at all times to secure the lowest possible rate of inflation. In situations in which the two objectives clash, the self-confidence with which the leadership of the Bundesbank makes use of its autonomy then plays a considerable role; and the history of the Bundesbank has been characterised by a particularly high degree of such self-confidence.

As has already been pointed out, that was true of the President of the Bank deutscher Länder, Wilhelm Vocke, who during the 1950's stood out against the financial policies desired by the Federal government.   But his successor as president of the Bundesbank, Karl Blessing, also clashed with those advocating an expansive employment policy in 1966/67, the period of the first larger-scale recession in the economic history of the Federal Republic.   The conflicts intensified sharply during the seventies, however, when increasing difficulties in maintaining economic growth led to more insistent calls for the state to adopt policies to stimulate employment.[23] As in all other Western countries, the government at first sought to operate a Keynesian-type fiscal policy and in doing so greatly enlarged the public debt, while the Bundesbank persisted in its policy of restricting the growth of the money supply. After the collapse of the Bretton Woods system and the introduction of flexible exchange rates against the dollar, it had adopted in 1973, certainly at least in part because of the ever-widening influence which monetarism was acquiring, a strategy of controlling monetary aggregates. That does not mean that the Bundesbank now conducted a monetarist policy (on this, see the later chapters), but it did seek to sustain the pressures for domestic adjustment to external disturbances - especially the first oil crisis - by following a policy which was restrictive when compared to that of the other important central banks. Underlying its actions was the correct view that what was involved in this situation was not a "demand shock" but a "supply shock". The noteworthy feature of the entire period was that the Bundesbank maintained its opposition to expansive fiscal policy under both the Social Democratic Bundesbank president Karl Klasen and his successor Karl Otto Pohl, who took up his post in 1980 after also serving as a member of the Federal government (from 1977 to 1980, Otmar Emminger was the Bank's president).

In general, it may be concluded that the Bundesbank's consistent pursuit of stability was made possible to a decisive extent by its wide-reaching autonomy and its continuous use of it. The fact that the Federal Republic has always been among the countries with the lowest rate of inflation is therefore largely due to the structure of its central bank, since the longer-term divergencies in inflation rates as between different countries can very probably be explained in terms of the greater or lesser degree of autonomy possessed by their respective central banks. Naturally, a further explanation is provided by the particular negative experience with inflation that Germany has had, so that in the minds of the public, and hence in government policy, the maintenance of the purchasing power of money has been afforded a higher rank as compared to other goals of economic policy than is the case in other countries. Nevertheless the rate of unemployment in the Federal Republic remained relatively low until the end of the seventies.

IV Functions and Duties of the Bundesbank

Similarly to the previous Reichsbank, but also to the important central banks of other countries, the Bundesbank performs four fundamental tasks:

1. As the central bank of issue, it has the monopoly of note issue, and regulates the supply of central bank money to the economy.

2. As the "bankers' bank", it is responsible
    for the solvency of the overall banking
    system.   In addition, in conjunction
    with the credit institutions it transacts
    a large proportion of payments in the
    Federal Republic.
3. As the state's bank, it is the "house bank"
    of the Federal government and - to a lesser
    extent - of the Länder as well.   In this
    function it performs payments transactions
    on behalf of the state and collaborates
    with the state in its borrowing.
4. Finally, the Bundesbank is the foreign
    currency bank of the Federal Republic: it
    administers Germany's currency reserves and
    looks after the interests and the duties of
    the Federal Republic in the organisations
    of the international monetary system.

As is the case with other central banking systems, the provision of the Federal Republic's
economy with central bank money comes from three
main sources: state borrowing from the central
bank ("fiscal components"), by the private banking
system from the central bank ("refinancing component"), and foreign indebtedness to the central bank
("foreign component").   The share of each of these
three components in the overall supply of central
bank money is, however, different in the Federal
Republic from other countries: by far the most
significant contribution is made by the foreign
components, with the other two of clearly lesser
significance (cf the following presentation of the
changes in the Bundesbank's balance sheet during the
period 1950-1980).   In the USA and Great Britain,
on the other hand, the refinancing and fiscal
components play a much greater role in the origins
of central bank money.   The Federal Republic's
particularity in this respect is due to the relatively large share of foreign trade in its national
product and the fact that its balance of payments
has for most of the period been in surplus.   Until
the beginning of the seventies, there were as well
substantial capital inflows in connection with
speculation on the upvaluation of the DM.   The
refinancing component became of greater importance
only in the later seventies.   (The later chapter on
Monetary Policy will analyse in more detail the
problems created for monetary policy by this one-

Table 2.2 : The Assets and Liabilities of the Deutsche Bundesbank, 1950-1980

(1) Assets

End-Year	Foreign Component		Refinancing Component		Fiscal Component[1]		Other Assets[2]		Total	
	Mrd. DM	%	Mrd. DM	%	Mrd. DM	%	Mrd. DM	%	Mrd. DM	%
1950	1079	6.2	5570	32.0	9206	52.9	1557	8.9	17412	100
1960	33242	73.8	1942	4.3	8849	19.6	1019	2.3	45052	100
1970	51338	60.5	18738	22.1	11093	13.1	3721	4.3	84890	100
1980	104382	53.3	57554	29.4	11120	5.7	22652	11.6	195708	100

(2) Liabilities

End-Year	Note Circulation[3]		Public Author-ities' Deposits		Deposits of Credit Institutions[4]		Other Liabilities[5]		Total	
	Mrd. DM	%	Mrd. DM	%	Mrd. DM	%	Mrd. DM	%	Mrd. DM	%
1950	8232	47.3	2550	14.6	1888	10.8	4742	27.2	17412	100
1960	20471	25.4	2859	6.3	13046	29.0	8676	19.3	45052	100
1970	36480	43.0	6726	7.9	26250	30.9	15434	18.2	84890	100
1980	83730	42.8	1015	0.5	53845	27.5	57118	29.2	195708	100

Source: Monthly Reports of the Deutsche Bundesbank and own calculations.

Notes: 1. Only lending to the Federal government.
2. Loans to firms, and securities' holdings and other assets.
3. Coin not included.
4. Predominantly minimum reserve deposits.
5. Provisions, reserves, basic capital, obligations from money market paper.

sided structure of the origin of central bank money.)

The note circulation is the significant component of the Bundesbank's liabilities.   In
absolute terms it about quadrupled during the
seventies, but declined a little as a proportion of
the Bundesbank's obligations.   The same is true of
the ratio of note and coin circulation to national
product, which almost quintupled during the same
period.   In addition to the note and coin circulation, the only Bank liabilities of significance are
the deposits of the credit institutes.   Essentially
they consist of their minimum reserve obligations,
for the minimum reserve ratio policy is - as in the
USA - one of the important instruments for controlling the use made of central bank money.

The Bundesbank's function as "bankers' bank"
naturally arises from one of its functions, that
of providing the credit institutions with central
bank money.   In addition to that supplied via the
components described above, the Bank makes money
available for adjustment purposes in particular
situations of need by intervening in the money market,
thus acting as "lender of last resort" (cf the later
description of the features of the money market in
the Federal Republic).   It also performs a large
part of payments business for the credit institutes
and the state, in line with the provision in the
Bundesbank Law that it should "attend to the conduct
of payments business through the banking system, both
at home and abroad".   In 1981, about 30% of the
orders to make payments accepted by the credit
institutions was performed by the Bank and for this
purpose it maintains a computer centre in every
Land.[25]   Finally, the Bank collaborates with the
Federal Office for the Supervision of the Credit
System in supervising the banks.   Any regulation
laid down by the Federal Supervisory Office requires
the agreement of the Bank.

While the Bank conducts extensive business on
behalf of the state, in doing so it is subject - in
line with the principle of autonomy - to precise,
restrictive conditions.   In particular, the state
has little possibility of borrowing from the Bank.
Only to finance short-term budget deficits, which
arise from disparities between current receipts and
expenditures during the budget period, can the
Federal government and those of the Länder take up
socalled cash advances from the Bank.   According to
section 20 of the Bundesbank Law, such advances to
the federal government are subject to a maximum of
6 Mrd. DM, and this limit cannot be exceeded.   So

far as concerns other forms of borrowing by the
Federal government, the Bank merely acts as its
"fiscal agent", i.e. it purchases on account of the
Federal government that authority's own long-term
bonds (financing bonds, Federal savings bonds and
Federal Bonds).   With respect to other public loans,
the Bank fulfills an advisory and coordinating role
and acts as leader in consortia formed to buy
Federal loans, without being thereby obliged to take
up a certain proportion of the new issues, as are
the other banks which are consortium members.   It
does, however, have the task of providing support
for the market in Federal loans, and to this end it
intervenes in the market to prevent especially sharp
fluctuations in their prices.

Finally, the Bank is responsible to a considerable extent for the preparation of official
statistics and information as to economic developments in the monetary sector.   It is no exaggeration to say that the monetary statistics of the
Federal Republic are among the most comprehensive
available anywhere in this area.   The Bank publishes Monthly Reports containing detailed
statistical appendices on current monetary developments;   these are supplemented by the socalled
Statistical Supplements in which seasonally -
adjusted time series and diagrams relating to
lengthier periods are presented.   In addition, at
less frequent intervals socalled Special Papers are
published by the Bank, in which are to be found
extensive statistical material relating to particular
matters of interest, e.g. the flow of funds analysis
for the overall economy or the balance of private
firms.

The important function which the Bank performs
as the "foreign-currency bank" stems from the significance of foreign trade to the Federal Republic.
The Bank administers the country's currency reserves,
which basically consist of holdings of dollars
(36.5 Mrd. DM at end-1981) and gold (13.7 Mrd. DM).
20% of these reserves were transferred to the
European Monetary Cooperation Fund (EMCF) when the
European Monetary System (EMS) was founded in 1979.
As compared to the gold and dollar reserves, claims
on the IMF (inclusive of Special Drawing Rights) are
of only small amount.   In the following table,[26]
the composition of the external position of the Bank
is given:

Table 2.3: Foreign Assets and Liabilities of the Bundesbank

Mrd. DM

	End – 1980	End – 1981
A. Currency Reserves	77.8	76.7
Gold	13.7	13.7
Foreign Currencies and Foreign Notes & Coin	42.6	37.3
Reserve Position in IMF and Special Drawing Rights	8.1	9.2
Claims on the EMCF within the framework of the EMS	35.9	39.9
Less:		
Sums arising from the valuation of the gold & dollar reserves temporarily transferred to the ECMF	-22.5	-23.4
B. Liabilities to non-residents	-14.4	-11.4
C. Net Currency Reserves	63.4	65.3
D. Credits to and other claims on non-residents	4.0	3.6
E. Net Foreign Assets	67.4	68.9
Overall Balance Sheet Total of Bundesbank	195.7	196.3

The Deutsche Bundesbank

The Bank's interventions in the foreign exchange market have certainly become considerably less frequent since the floating of exchange rates and the collapse of the Bretton Woods system, but after all it is only a "dirty float" that has taken place. Thus in 1977 and 1978, when foreign funds were switched from the dollar into the DM, the Bank purchased foreign currency to an amount of 30 Mrd. DM. In addition, within the framework of the so-called European currency snake (since 1972) and then later in the EMS (since 1979) the Bank has committed itself to maintaining the parities agreed upon with the other members, and this has necessitated regular interventions in the foreign exchange market. We shall return to this aspect in more detail in later chapters.

NOTES

1. In this connection, see especially K.V. Bonin, Zentralbanken zwischen funktioneller Unabhängigkeit und politischer Autonomie - dargestellt an der Bank von England, der Bank von Frankreich und der Deutschen Bundesbank, Baden-Baden 1979. For historical details, pp. 26-89 of this work.
2. The Prussian Bank was formed in 1847 on the basis of the Royal Giro and Lehnbank set up in 1765 by Frederick II, so that the latter institution was in strict terms the forefunner of the Reichsbank.
3. At the end of 1873, the volume of bank notes in circulation in the overall area of the Reich was about 1350 Mill. Marks. Almost 900 millions of that had been issued by the Prussian Bank, 80 Millions by other Prussian note-issuing banks, and 370 Millions by banks in the other German states. See Bonin, op. cit., p. 64, and G.V. Eynern, Die Reichsbank, Jena 1928, p.6
4. The most eminent advocate of a new central bank was Ludwig Bamberger. For his speeches on this subject, see Eynern, op. cit., P. 13
5. According to the law No. 745 of 4 December 1871, a Mark corresponded to 1/2790 kg. of fine gold; in England, the value of the pound was set at 1/137 kg. fine gold.
6. W. Stutzel, Währung in weltoffener Wirtschaft, Frankfurt A.M., 1973, ch. 12 pp.183-187, and R. Stucken, Deutsche Geld und Kreditpolitik 1914-1953, Tübingen 1953, p. 14
7. Bonin, op. cit., pp. 68ff

8. H.J. Schacht, Die Stabilisierung der Mark, Berlin/Leipzig 1927, p. 84

9. H.J. Arndt, Politik und Sachverstand im Kreditwährungsgesetz, Berlin 1963, p. 101

10. The General Council consisted of 14 members, of which seven had to be German citizens and seven be foreign citizens. The Board of Directors was nominated by the General Council, and one of the foreign members of the Council was chosen as Commissioner for Note Issue.

11. The stabilization of the Reichsmark which then followed has been ascribed above all to the efforts of Schacht, although his appointment met with some resistance among the other members of the Board of Directors and the Reich government. Cf. H. Müller, Die Zentralbank - eine Gegenregierung. Reichsbankpräsident Hjalmar Schacht als Politiker der Weimarer Republik, Opladen 1973

12. H.H. Hansmeyer & R. Caeser, "Kriegswirtschaft und Inflation (1936-1948)", in: Deutsche Bundesbank (ed.), Währung und Wirtschaft in Deutschland, Frankfurt A.M., 1976, pp. 367ff

13. E. Wandel, Die Entstehung der Bank deutscher Länder und die deutsche Währungsreform 1948, Frankfurt A.M., 1980, presents a detailed and interesting history of the reorganisation of the German central banking system after the Second World War.

14. Noteworthy in this connection is that the essential negotiations in the preparation of the currency reform were conducted on the American side by a young Army lieutenant, Edward E. Tenenbaum.

15. Cf. the detailed presentation in Wandel, op. cit., pp. 48ff

16. Of interest in this context is the relatively high degree of continuity in the leading personnel of the German central banks: the last president of the Prussian Bank, von Dechend, became the first Reichsbank president in 1875. The president of the Reichsbank that had been appointed by the Kaiser remained in office throughout the war and for the first five years of the Weimar Republic. His successor Hjalmar Schacht also filled the position until 1939 in the Third Reich. Similarly, Wilhelm Vocke, the president of the Bank deutscher Länder, and Karl Blessing, who succeeded him as president of the Bundesbank, had already belonged to the Board of Directors of the Reichsbank under Schacht. See Bonin, op. cit., pp. 85ff

17.   The Board of Directors of the Bank deutscher
Länder was the executive organ of the Bank.   It
consisted of the President, his deputy and several
other members, with the President being elected by
the Central Bank Council.   The Central Bank Council
in turn was composed of the Bank's Board of
Directors together with the presidents of the 11
associated Land central banks and an elected chair-
man.   Finally, the presidents of the Land central
banks were named by the respective Land governments,
although they then had no right to issue instructions
to them.   Until 1951, the Allied Banking Commission
had a right of veto over the Bank's decisions.
18.   Because of the autonomy with which he
conducted the Bank's policy, Vocke repeatedly came
into conflict with Adenauer.   In particular, Vocke
successfully resisted demands for an expansion of
the money supply.
19.   The subordination of other goals of
economic policy, especially those relating to
employment and economic growth, to that of maintaining the purchasing power of money was not, in the
dominant view, placed in question by the socalled
Law on Stability and Growth passed in 1967.   For
the requirement that it contained, i.e. that the
Bank should "through the policy it conducted
simultaneously contribute to the stabilization of
the price level, a high level of employment and
external equilibrium together with a steady and
appropriate growth rate", had to take account of
the "duties incumbent upon it".   And the primary
duty of the Bank is the safeguarding of the
currency" according to section 3 of the Bundesbank
Law.   On this, see Bonin, op. cit., pp. 175ff
20.   Nevertheless, the question as to whether
the autonomy of the Bank does not contradict the
principle of democratic decision-making has never
ceased to be an object of discussion.   Such
disputes have intensified in the situations in which
there have been serious conflicts between the Bank
and the Federal government;   in the pages which
follow, some attention is given to these conflicts.
21.   The diagram is drawn from the very informative Sonderdruck No. 7 of the Deutschen Bundesbank,
Die Deutsche Bundesbank, May 1982.
22.   Of the nine members of the Board of
Directors of a Federal Reserve Bank, six are chosen
by the member banks, while 3 are appointed by the
Board of Governors.   The differing views of the
individual Federal Reserve Banks as to the appropriate monetary policy can also be attributed to the

relatively high degree of independence they possess. Well-known in this context is _e.g._ the demand for a monetarist monetary policy voiced by the Federal Reserve Bank of St. Louis at the end of the 'sixties in opposition to the Board of Governors. An open disagreement of this type between representatives of the central banking system is scarcely conceivable in the Federal Republic.

23. Cf. u.a. H.H. Francke, "Konsistenzprobleme der Geld- und Fiskalpolitik in den 70er Jahren", _in_: W. Ehrlicher & D.B. Simmert (eds.), _Geld und Währungspolitik in der Bundesrepublik Deutschland_, Beiheft 7 zur "Kredit und Kapital", 1983

24. Extracted from _Die Deutsche Bundesbank_, Sonderdruck der Deutschen Bundesbank, No. 7 May 1982, p.10

25. _Ibid._, p. 20
26. _Ibid._, p. 25

Chapter 3

THE CREDIT INSTITUTIONS IN THE FEDERAL REPUBLIC OF
GERMANY

The structure of the banking system in the Federal
Republic of Germany is characterised by two features
which together distinguish it from that in other
countries: first, the dominance of the socalled
"universal bank"; and secondly, its division into
three about equally strong sectors, those of the
private banks, the public banks and the cooperative
banking sector.

    The dominance of the universal bank has contri-
buted substantially to the efficiency and the
economic power of the German credit system.   Yet
their power has been able to be controlled through
both market competition and state and/or decentra-
lised elements of control.   The latter has been
exercised by legal regulation and government
supervisory bodies; but it is above all the actual
division of the system into private and commercial
banks, public and cooperative banking agencies,
between which intensive competition is the rule,
that has eased the task of control.

    In what follows, these structural elements will
firstly be more fully explained.   Then the most
important groups of credit institutions will be
presented in detail, and finally significant legal
regulations and the supervision of the banks
exercised by the state will be outlined.

I Basic Structural Characteristics

1. The Universal Bank
The type of bank known as the "universal bank" is
characteristic of the German banking system in
particular and the overall financial system in
general.   As opposed to the banks specialized by
activity which are dominant in other countries -

44

above all Anglo-Saxon countries - universal banks
conduct every type of banking business "under the
one roof".   Thus, they lend on short-term and long-
term; carry out business in securities, direct
investment in other firms, and foreign business;
and draw their financial resources from time
deposits, savings certificates and bank bonds.
Hence they can offer their customers all types of
banking services "at the one counter", while in e.g.
Britain, the homeland of the system of credit
institutions specialised by function, firms in
general must call upon the services both of a
financially-strong clearing bank and also of a
merchant bank skilled in the knowledge of financing
know-how.[1]
     The universal banks are consequently highly
efficient.   Without the assistance of specialized
banks, they are able to perform all the services
required by large-scale diversified firms as their
"house bank", and they can easily adjust themselves
to changes in such firms' financing needs and modes
of operation.   Their ability in these directions
has led to the formation of close relationships
between individual banks and their customers, and
often also to cross-linkages of ownership between
them.   Thereby encouraged is the continuous growth
of the individual banks, which often can arrive via
concentration at a certain degree of power over
other spheres of the economy.   In this way, certain
disadvantages or even dangers of the universal bank
are simultaneously highlighted: possibly an excessive degree of influence over other firms and the
state, or even a misuse of the power they possess;
a reduction of competition in the financial system
through concentration; and the accumulation of
financial risks at individual banks.[2]
     For this reason, there has been no lack of
critics at home and abroad to repeatedly point to
the problems involved in the German system of
universal banking, and to demand that restrictions
be placed upon its development or even that it be
eliminated altogether.   Such criticism has led to
amendments being made to the legislation covering
banking, but also in 1974 to the setting-up by the
Federal Finance Minister of a Study Commission to
look into "Basic Questions Relating to the Credit
System".   Its task was primarily to examine the
problems associated with the universal type of bank.
In the foreground of its concern stood, firstly,
questions of the conflict of interest that could
arise between a universal bank and its customers

when the former was simultaneously active in both
the deposit and lending business on the one hand
and the sale of securities on the other.   Secondly,
there was the danger that might arise of concent-
rations of economic power among particular credit
institutes because of their holdings in other (non-
banking) companies, their right to vote the shares
deposited with them by their customers, and their
dominance of particular markets for credit and for
securities.

The Commission submitted its Final Report in
1979 (Schriftenreihe of the Federal Ministry of
Finance, Vol. 28).   Though the exhaustive analysis
it had undertaken did not permit it to reject as
completely unfounded the fears noted above, its
final conclusion represented the views of an overwhelming majority of its members that, in the vast
majority of cases, the criticism of the universal
banks had been excessive.   The advantages of the
system of universal banks, it argued, clearly out-
weighed its disadvantages, and hence it should not
be given up in favour of a system of banks specialised by function.   Yet the Commission's work not
merely pointed out in great detail the possible
dangers of the system, dangers to which we shall
later have to return on several occasions, but also
analysed their relevance for future banking
legislation.

These dangers certainly provide positive
arguments for the Anglo-Saxon system of banks
specialized by function, and also played a significant role in the American demands after the Second
World War that the large banks should be decentra-
lised and their head offices eliminated (the Dodge
Plan of 5 October 1945).   Another element in such
demands was that the large banks had been incrimin-
ated in the Third Reich through their financing of
the war and personal entanglement with the Nazi
leadership.[3]   It was due to British influence that
nevertheless the universal bank continued to exist
in the Federal Republic and could continue its long
historical tradition.   For the British believed
that a decentralization of the banking system and
its specialization by function would render Allied
control more difficult, encourage local monopolies
and make the German economy in general more subject
to fluctuation.   Certainly, with British agreement
the large banks were decentralized on 1 April 1948,
but the universal bank survived.   When the
restrictions on the formation of branches were
abolished by the Large Banks Law of 1952 and 1956,

the successors of the three large banks (Deutsche
Bank, Dresdner Bank and Commerzbank) could merge
together again.   The question is therefore raised
as to whether the dangers of the universal banking
system outlined above have in fact shown themselves
in the post-war development of the German banking
system.

2. Concentration, Interlinking and International-
ization

What needs to be established first of all is that
the German banking system grew extremely rapidly
after the Currency Reform of 1949.   The total
deposits of all banks (excluding building societies
and the central bank) rose from 39.1 Mrd. DM in 1950
to 252.5 Mrd. DM in 1960, then to 817.9 Mrd. DM in
1970, and finally to 2538.4 Mrd. DM in 1981.[4]
Hence it grew 65-fold during a period when the
nominal value of Gross National Product rose by only
about 16-fold.   One reason for this disproportional-
ly rapid growth is to be found in the rising demand
for bank services in general, a feature that can be
observed in other countries as well.   Yet at the
same time it also reflects a particular characteristic of the German banking and financial system,
namely that the proportion of the financing of
overall economic activities that it performs is
extremely high by international standards.   An
especially intensive degree of financial intermediation is therefore to be found in the Federal
Republic.   Its causes lie, first, in the scale of
post-war reconstruction, which was financed above
all by credit - particularly in the field of
housing - and the relatively large share of foreign
trade in national income, which makes great use of
services provided by the banks.   Secondly, German
firms rely upon credit to a clearly greater degree
than firms in other countries.   And finally, during
the 1970's a very rapid rise in state indebtedness
has taken place, and state debt issues are handled
mostly by the banks.   (In the following chapter,
the particular features and problems of the aggregate
flows of funds in the Federal Republic will be
discussed in greater detail.)

The growth of the credit institutions and their
general activity in intermediation has been accompanied by a pronounced increase in the degree of
concentration in banking, a process which picked up
pace in the 1960's and has still not come to an end.
As a result, the number of credit institutions has
declined from 13359 in 1957 to 5355 in 1980.   The

number of their offices has simultaneously risen by about 60%: in 1957 the individual credit institution possessed an average of two offices, in 1980 almost nine. This development is shown in detail in the table 3.1 on the following page.[5]

For several reasons, however, the expansion in the bank office network may now be regarded as over; in fact, many people are expecting an actual decline in the number of branches in the future. For a start, the level of population has stagnated and there has been a decline in housing construction. But above all, the conduct of payments transactions and the provision of banking services will undoubtedly experience considerable technical improvements in the future, and hence restrict the need for an expansion of the bank office network with its associated high personnel cost. Representatives of the banking industry frequently complain that the Federal Republic is "overbanked"; but while that seems an exaggeration at present, it may be accepted as pointing to a situation that could actually be realized in future.

Along with the growth in and concentration of the German credit system has gone an intensification of its links with business enterprises. Thus, the Study Commission whose Report has been referred to above presented the following results from its research: with respect to 74 large enterprises quoted on the stock exchange in 1974/75, credit institutions in aggregate: owned 9% of the capital stock; represented on average more than 62% of the votes in the stockholders' meetings; and held 18% of the seats on the supervisory boards. One reason for such a high degree of interlinkage is the large degree to which German firms rely on outside financing, but as well the direct participation by banks in such firms· has continuously increased.[6] This latter development can be traced in turn to three factors: firstly, the close ties between individual firms and their "house banks" have often led to the credit institute concerned taking up a direct interest in the firm, with the aim of receiving a share in its direction and control of it. Secondly, in order to extend their activities into new fields of financial intermediary business, such as leasing, trust companies and investment funds, the banks have often acquired interests in companies already operating in such fields.[7] Thirdly, and above all in the '70s, the banks have also become involved in certain firms in the public interest, either to safeguard jobs under reorganization

The Credit Institutions

Table 3.1

End-Year	Credit Institutions	Branch Offices	Total Bank Offices	Change in Total Bank Offices
1957	13359	12974	26333	—
1965	11836	23046	35955	+ 9622
1975	6487	37103	43590	+ 7635
1980	5355	39311	44666	+ 1076

schemes or to prevent foreign interests from obtaining a majority stake in German firms. Yet, more significant than these for the links between firms and banks are two factors which are not reflected in banks' actually acquiring participations in businesses. Thus a large proportion of the seats on the supervisory boards of public limited companies are filled by representatives of the credit institutions. But in addition to this, the majority of the small shareholders authorize the banks who administer the shares they have deposited with them to represent them at shareholders' general meetings, so that the banks can actually cast a majority vote at such meeting.[8]

Given these factors, it can be concluded with complete certainty that the banks exert upon German business firms an influence which goes far beyond their basic function as financial intermediaries. Yet this influence is bound up with the assumption of considerable risks, since as the owners of the risk capital the banks become involved to an especial degree in changes in the earnings of the firms. Hence in the Federal Republic, in distinction from prevailing conditions in the USA or Britain, it is the banks who bear a significant share of business risks. This creates important tasks for the Federal Banking Supervisory Office and necessitates special legal regulations, which will be discussed in the final part of this chapter.

Finally, particular risks have also arisen from the internationalization of banking business stemming from the growth of German foreign trade and above all from the creation of the large "offshore" financial markets, especially the Euromarket. The years from 1973 to 1980 alone witnessed almost a tripling of the number of foreign branches and subsidiaries of German credit institutions, with an even larger rise in their volume of business.

Most important in this context are the banking centres of Luxembourg and London and thus dealings in the Euromarket. The dominant business is in socalled "roll-over" credits, which are also extended in greater volume to developing countries and the East European centrally planned economies. Most "roll-over" credits bear an interest rate which is subject to annual adjustment, with the result that any risk of changes in that rate are one-sidedly imposed upon the borrower. To insure against the risk of the borrowers' becoming insolvent, a number of Euro-banks normally participate in the individual commitment to lend. Since the Euro-

branches and affiliates of the German credit institutions have only a very small amount of funds at
their own disposal, the actual risk (a risk that is
not infrequently considerable and has risen significantly since the oil crises) is borne by the German
mother bank.   It is therefore very significant that
the German Bank Supervisory Authority has intensified
its efforts in recent years to draw these foreign
risks into its sphere of control.[9]   Table 3.2
again shows the rapid expansion of the foreign
activity of the German credit institutions.[10]

3. The Three-Sector System

If there has been no misuse of the power that the
credit instiutions have gained in the Federal
Republic through concentration and the interlinkages
between them, that is due above all to the three-
sector nature of the banking system, a characteristic
stemming from its historical development.   It has
ensured that intensive competition has been maintained.   What is meant by a three-sector system is
simply that the banking system in the Federal
Republic is made up of three large sectors, differing from each other in their legal form, forms of
ownership and their aims, but competing with each
other as universal banks in all sections of the
financial market and transacting through particular
organisational forms a comparable amount of business
in each section of that market.   Hence the market
strength they each possess ensures the maintenance
of a high degree of workable competition between
them.   The three sectors are, then, the group of
private and commercial banks;   the public banks,
especially the savings banks and central giro
institutions (i.e. regional central institutions of
the savings banks);   and finally the credit
cooperatives.
     The group of commercial and private banks
embraces four types of credit institutions: the
large commercial banks, regional banks, private
banking firms and the branches of foreign banks.
They are private-law corporations under the ownership of private individuals or firms, and basically
profit-orientated in their operations.   Savings
banks and their central giro institutions, on the
other hand, are public-law institutions under state
ownership and basically pursue a public purpose
orientated towards the common welfare.   The
individual savings banks are restricted in the

Table 3.2

	End-Year		
	1973	1977	1980
Institutions with foreign branches	10	15	16
Number of branches	23	47	74
Volume of Business done by branches (Mrd. DM)	15	47.0	94.9
Foreign subsidiaries	27	35	52

business they can do, both by being confined to
certain regions and by being prevented from engaging
in certain types of business.   But the institutions
in which they are associated at the Land level, the
central giro institutions and Landesbanken, are not
subject to such restrictions and thus can compete in
all markets as universal banks of considerable size.
The credit co-operatives originated as public self-
help organizations for agriculture and crafts, but
have likewise joined together to form large central
banks.   As shareholders in them, their customers
are simultaneously their owners (Volks- and Raiffeisenbanken), hence their operating policy is geared
to the interests of their members.   In addition to
these "three pillars" of the German system, there
are other banks specialising in particular fields,
above all the real estate credit banks and - mostly
under public ownership - institutions set up to
fulfill particular needs, and some of them are of
considerable significance in their particular
spheres of activity.
        The tripartite nature of the German banking
system has not merely been significant with respect
to the maintenance of competition.   It has also
enabled it to fulfill the important function of
providing a range of banking services diversified
both regionally and by types of customer.   The
consideration of public goals and interests has been
ensured without the principles of the market having
been thereby basically neglected.   In its structure,
therefore, the banking system has tended to approach
the model of a mixed, socially responsible economic
system, with market mechanisms of guidance and
control, that finds overwhelming support in the
Federal Republic.   The demand for nationalization
of the banks that in other countries, e.g. France,
has always been raised by socialist political parties
has been of little significance in the Federal
Republic because large parts of the credit system
are already in public ownership and/or operate
according to the principle of public benefit.
Conversely, the competition between such institutions
and the private banks, and the refusal of the
relevant state authorities to exercise any permanent
direct influence upon the operating policy of
publicly-owned credit institutions, has prevented
the economic inefficiences that might otherwise
emerge.
        Before the most important institutions in the
German banking system are discussed in detail, the
following table 3.3 is presented[11] to show the

relative significance of the individual banking groups. With respect to the three sector structure of the system, the market share of each group is as follows:
- private and commercial banks: 20.89%;
- (publicly-owned) savings banks and regional central institutions of public savings banks: 38.49%;
- cooperative banks: 16.39%;
- other institutions with special functions: 23.69%.

This list does not include the building societies, which are of considerable importance in the Federal Republic in the financing of housing construction.

Table 3. : Banking Groups and their Total Business
(as at end-1981)

Banking Groups	Mrd. DM	In %'age of all banking groups
Commercial Banks	578.9	22.8
The Big 3	228.1	9.0
Regional and other Commercial Banks	262.0	10.3
Branches of Foreign Banks	51.8	2.0
Private Banks	37.0	1.5
Regional central institutions of public savings banks (incl. Deutsche Girozentrale)	418.5	16.5
Public Savings Banks	555.2	21.9
Cooperative Central Banks (incl. Deutsche Genossenschaftsbank)	103.2	4.0
Credit Cooperatives	283.6	1.2
(Credit Cooperatives including institutions not obliged to submit reports)[1]	(310.0)	(12.3)
Real Estate Credit Institutions	358.4	14.1
Private mortgage banks	220.0	8.7
Public mortgage banks	138.4	5.4
Instalment Credit Companies	29.7	1.2
Credit Institutions with specialised tasks	169.2	6.7
Postal Cheque Offices and Postal Savings Banks	41.7	1.6
TOTAL FOR ALL BANKING GROUPS[2]	2538.4	100.00

1. Balance sheet totals; figures for total business volume not available.
2. All the institutes reporting to the banking statistics office (not including Building Societies).
The individual figures do not sum to the total because of rounding-off.

The Credit Institutions

II The Individual Groups

1. Private Commercial Banks
The most important private commercial banks are the
so called Big Three: the Deutsche Bank, the
Dresdner Bank, and the Commerzbank. They have
certain features in common: the post-war experience
they shared of deconcentration and subsequent re-
amalgamation; the image they present to the public,
with a branch network covering the whole of the
Federal Republic; a similar business structure;
and shared success at their efforts to "go international". Each of the Big Three was set up in
the period around 1871, the founding years of the
Reich, and built up their position of leadership
among the private commercial banks by mergers above
all in the 1920's and 30's. After their deconcentration and splitting-up into regional organisations by the Allied Occupation forces, they were
then re-amalgamated in 1956. Since then they
have grown rapidly, and have sought to effect a
broad distribution of their shares among the public
and their employees and abroad. In mid-1980, the
distribution was as shown in table 3.4[13]
     The significance of the big banks[14] lies less
in the extent of business they do than in the fact
that they play a leading role in the financing of
foreign trade and of industry. Thus, they are
responsible for just on 50% of the foreign trade
dealings of the German banking system, and about a
half of national and international security issuing
business. The same is true of equity and other
investment in non-banking companies, where the three
big banks have the largest share. To these activities was added a new one in the 1970's, as trade
with the East European countries expanded, although
such involvement has brought considerable risks with
it, e.g. with respect to Poland and Rumania. Finally, the big banks have increasingly sought to
penetrate into the mass deposit business, that
concerned with current accounts and saving deposits,
a field that has traditionally been dominated by the
savings banks. It was mainly to this end that they
rapidly expanded their branch network during the
70's.
     In addition to the "Big Three", there are a few

Table 3.4

	Number of Shareholders	Of whom, Employees	Proportion of shares held abroad
Commerzbank	130,000	15,000	15%
Deutsche Bank	205,000	38,000	22%
Dresdner Bank	145,000	24,000	20%

regional banks of particular significance among the
private commercial banks: especially the Bavarian
limited liability banks, the Bayerische Hypotheken -
und Wechselbank and the Bayerische Vereinsbank.
Although their business activity was previously
restricted to Bavaria, they have spread into the
whole of the Federal Republic and also abroad since
the 60's, so that their categorization as "regional
banks" in actuality now merely reflects the concentration of their branch network in a particular
region.   There are two other large concerns class-
ified as regional banks, though they too have
branches throughout Germany and abroad as well: the
Bank für Gemeinwirtschaft (BfG) owned by the trade
unions, and the Berliner Handels-und Frankfurter
Bank (BHF-Bank).
       The oldest group among the commercial banks,
but with respect to its volume of business now the
smallest, are the so-called Privatbankiers.   Their
history stretches back to medieval times, when large
merchant houses went over to transacting money
changing and lending business for their customers
and later specialized in these fields.   Given the
large capital sums required in the financing of
German industrialisation in the 19th century, as
well as the bank crashes of the 1920's and 30's,
the number of these private banks has continually
declined.   Thus in 1925 there were still 1406 of
them in the German Reich, 493 in 1941, but only 83
at the end of 1980, and even many of these belonged
to other banks.   As opposed to the big banks and
the savings banks, the private banks are not involved in the mass deposit business but specialise above
all in the flotation of and dealings in securities,
where very personal relationships to a few large
clients often exist.   Hence, though much smaller
in the volume of business they do than the merchant
banks in Britain, they possess certain similarities
to them.   Significant among these private banks are
the Cologne banking house of Sal. Oppenheim Jr. &
Cie, a concern rich in tradition, and the Munich
private bank Merch, Finck & Co.   Since 1975 the
second largest private bank, Trinkaus & Burckhardt
in Düsseldorf, has been under the control of the
American Citybank.

2. The Savings Banks
Savings banks originated in Germany in the 18th
century.   They were set up above all to fulfill
aims of a social policy nature and it is from this
that the so-called public function of the savings

banks and their organisation was later derived.
This public function came to the forefront when
during the 19th century numerous savings banks were
founded by local government authorities, and played
an essential role in the financing of infrastructural
works in their respective localities.   Hence, from
their very beginning the savings bank contributed
significantly to regional development in Germany,
even if - in distinction from savings banks in
England and France - the German savings banks were
all but universal banks in their operations.   In
1850, there were already in Prussia alone 234 savings
banks, with deposits of over 18 million Thaler.[16]

In addition to their public function, the
provision of assistance to socially weak groups
among the population and the development of the
local infrastructure, an essential task of the
savings banks later became the conduct of mass payments transactions.   That was made possible by the
formation of giro associations, which even before
the First World War had effected payments on a
clearing basis between the individual savings banks
associated - though retaining their independence -
with them.   It was from the giro associations that
there developed the Landesbanken and central giro
institutions (Girozentralen), which were then
progressively built up into large universal banks.
In addition, the savings banks came together in
regional associations and in the German Savings
Banks and Giro Association, which performs advisory
functions for the savings banks, runs training
courses for their personnel and represents their
interests.

The business activity of the savings banks is
governed by a series of regulations laid down in the
savings banks' laws of the individual Länder.   By
far the most important of this is the so-called
guarantor obligation, i.e. the authority conducting
a savings bank (city or town, rural district council
or association of local government authorities) is
fully responsible (with public funds) for its
obligations.   On the other hand, the savings banks
are prohibited from involving themselves in certain
types of business, those of an especially risky
nature, e.g. speculative dealings in stocks and
shares.   The purpose is to maintain them in a
particularly solvent state, and in recompense they
operate on the basis of somewhat more liberal
provisions with respect to capital requirements than
other credit institutes.   Another characteristic of
the savings banks is the so-called "regional

principle", i.e. the regulation that restricts the business activity of individual savings banks by confining their setting-up of branches to particular regions.

The distinctive features of the savings banks is their dominant position in the bulk deposit business.   Savings deposits account for more than half their liabilities.   On the assets side, in addition to personal loans and mortgages finance it is naturally loans to local authorities which figure largest.   They contribute indirectly to financing local authorities' activities by either themselves acquiring from their Landesbanken or central giro institutions the bonds issued by the latter ("mortgage bonds" and "communal bonds") or by selling them on their behalf to their own customers. It is thus the savings banks who are the large scale assemblage points for the savings of the broad public, while the central bodies (the Landesbanken/ central giro institutions) perform the payments business and place the surplus liquidity of the savings banks in the capital and money markets.

The close cooperation between savings banks and their central giro institutions has been of great importance for the successful growth of the savings bank sector.   The central giro institutions have in the process increasingly developed into large universal banks which also play a significant role in international banking business.   Of greatest importance in this context are the Westdeutsche Landesbank - Girozentrale, the Bayerische Landesbank-Girozentrale and the Hessische Landesbank-Girozentrale.   The concentration process in the German banking system has also affected the savings bank sector, and in the 70's a few very large savings banks came into being (the Hamburg Savings Bank is one of the three largest savings banks in Europe) which, because of the volume of business they transact, are already loosening their traditionally close ties to their central giro institutions.   At the present time, however, there are still 611 savings banks with over 17000 offices throughout the whole of the Federal Republic.

3. The Cooperative Banks

Cooperative banks had already been set up at the beginning of the 19th century as self-help organisations for agriculture and the crafts.   Their basic principle was that of self-help through the lending of working capital, the funds for this purpose being raised from the amounts their members

had paid up on their shares in the cooperative.
Till recently, two large groups of credit cooperatives existed in Germany: those founded by
Friedrich-Wilhelm Raifeissen in 1846 and concentrating upon the credit needs of agriculturists; and
those owing their origin to Franz-Hermann Schulze
from Delitzsch, whose customers included craftsmen,
traders and the general public. It was only in
1972, after the two organisations had been locked
in often sharp competition with each other for over
a century, that they were organisationally unified
through the formation of the Bundesverband des
Deutschen Volksbanken and Raiffeisenbanken.

One of the most interesting features of the
cooperative banks is their embodiment of the goal
of self-help by encouraging the economic success of
their members. Initially this meant that it was
only their members who could be customers with them.
It was their deposits that formed the net worth of
the bank; they were also liable, after the socalled "addition in respect of members' uncalled
liability" had been taken into account, to "further
calls" of prescribed amount, i.e. they had to cover
from their own funds any losses made by the bank.
On the other hand, they shared in the bank's
profits in proportion to the volume of their shares
they held. Today, however, non-members too can be
customers at the banks, and the return on the
members' shares may take the form of either a fixed
interest rate or a proportional share of the profits
made.

Even though the overwhelming proportion of the
customers of the cooperative banks still come from
agriculture and small and medium-sized businesses,
the banks have developed into the most vigorous
competitors of the savings banks. As a result,
their business structure closely resembles that of
the savings banks: like the latter, obligations to
non-banks comprise the dominant share of their
liabilites, though a greater proportion of their
assets arises from transactions with credit
institutions, especially the cooperative central
banks with which they are associated.

As compared to the Landesbanken-central giro
institutions of the savings bank sector, the business activities of the individual cooperative central
banks is concentrated more upon the equalisation of
liquidity as between their member banks, the provision of services and the transmission of loans.
Their funds are overwhelmingly drawn (up to 80%)
from deposits by credit institutions with them and

loans from such institutions, above all the cooperative banks linked with them.   Only the Deutsche
Genossenschaftsbank, the leading institution of the
cooperative sector, displays more involvement in the
area of agricultural credit.

4. Other Credit Institutions with Specialized Functions

In addition to these "three pillars" of the German
credit system: the private commercial banks, the
savings banks and the cooperative sector, there are
a series of credit institutions with specialized
functions.   A distinction must be drawn between
three types of such institutions: first, those
concerned above all with the financing of public and
private construction activity; secondly, those
which undertake certain specialized public tasks;
and thirdly, those involved in the granting of consumer credit.   Such institutions are either directly under public ownership or frequently conduct
certain specialized activities for the private
commercial banks, the savings banks or the cooperative sector.
    Real estate credit institutions and building
societies concentrate upon private building activity
and borrowing by public authorities for this purpose.
Private and public mortgage banks belong to the
former category.   They both raise the funds to
finance their activities by the issue of particular
types of bonds, especially the so-called mortgage
bonds and communal bonds, for which specific regulations had already been set out in 1900.   So as to
facilitate the diminution of risk through an appropriate matching of the term structure of liabilities
and assets, special provisions were laid down for
certain institutions (among which, nevertheless, the
Landesbanken and central giro institutions are also
included) limiting to them the right to issue
mortgage and communal bonds.   Even if the regulations in the Mortgage Bank Law have been amended
several times since then, their basic content has
remained untouched up to the present day and confer
upon the real estate credit institutions a unique
market position.   After the Second World War they
were the dominant source of finance for the reconstruction of the housing stock.   Later, as
government indebtedness grew in the 70's, an even
greater portion of their activity lay in the
financing of that government debt.   But some real
estate credit institutions have also specialized
in the financing of shipbuilding, or have involved

themselves, within the framework of the European Community, with loans to foreign local government authorities; and to the extent that they are owned by larger branch banks and groups of financial institutions, they can utilize the closeness to customers of the branch networks of these institutions above all to dispose of their bonds.[18]

Of particular significance in the financing of housing construction in the Federal Republic are the building societies, which have been among the most rapidly expanding credit institutions in the post-war period. Similarly to the original self-help principle of the cooperative banks, the building societies too employ their deposits exclusively in the provision of housing loans at favourable interest rates to those saving through the societies.[19] The speedy reconstruction of the housing stock after the Second World War; the rising aspiration later on for individually occupied property; the considerable degree of encouragement to saving through building societies that the state has afforded (through tax concessions and premia for the building society savers); all these have been together responsible for the fact that the building societies as a whole could point to a balance sheet total of 132.5 Mrd. DM at the end of 1980. In addition to 13 publicly owned building societies, the very large majority of which operate as legally dependent departments of the Landesbanken - central giro institutions, there are 17 private, independent building societies.[20]

The public-law credit institutions with specialized functions are for the most part banks which were set up by the state after the First and Second World Wars in connection with attempts to overcome particular post-war problems. Four of these. institutions deserve special emphasis. First there is the Equalization of Burdens Bank (Lastenausgleichsbank), which was active in settling claims for damages arising from the war and in the integration of expellees and refugees into the West German economy.[21] The Reconstruction Loan Corporation (Kreditanstalt für Wiederaufbau) took on special importance in the rebuilding of the German economy. Founded in 1948/49, its task was originally to allocate the loans made available within the budget (the socalled ERP funds). Since then the Corporation has taken over a larger role in the banking arrangement of development aid. The German Land Settlement and Land Mortgage Bank (Deutsche Siedlungs-und Landesrentenbank) and the Agricultural Mortgage Bank (Landwirtschaftliche Rentenbank) play

an important role in the reorganisation of agricultural units and the provision of credit to agriculture
and forestry.   Finally, in a wider sense of credit
institutions with specialized functions there are
the Postal Cheque Offices and Postal Saving Banks.
They are publicly owned, legally dependent undertakings of the German Federal Post Office and concentrate upon the facilitation of payments transactions and the acceptance of savings deposits.

Like most of the other credit institutions, but
in this case almost exclusively, instalment credit
banks are engaged in the granting of consumer credit.
They are very largely subsidiaries of the large
commercial banks, in fact also of the "Big Three" of
the American banking system.   While the volume of
instalment credit extended ("small-scale lending"
and "medium sized consumer loans") had risen rapidly
since the 50's in the Federal Republic as well,
consumer credit in general plays a much smaller role
than in e.g. the USA.[22]   Borrowing of this type
frequently takes the form of overdrafts on salary
earners' bank accounts, a facility that all banks
either permit to their customers with relative
liberality or agree right from the beginning to
extend to them (socalled "overdraft facilities").

To conclude, a picture of the structure of the
German Banking system may be given as follows in
table 3.5.[23]

III Legal Framework and Bank Supervision

1. The Law on Banking
As in most other countries[24] the activity of the
banks is subjected to particular requirements and
regulations in addition to those imposed upon them
by general legislation.   The most important of these
provisions are embodied in the Law on Banking which
came into force in 1962.   Its immediate predecessor
in the field was the "Reich Banking Law", drawn up
in 1934 in reaction to the great banking crisis of
the immediately preceding period, and summarizing
and significantly elaborating the numerous individual regulations that had hitherto existed.   The
Banking Law of 1961 underwent substantial amendment
in 1976.[25]

If the provisions of that Law are compared with
those relating to banking in other countries, they
appear to be relatively liberal, because they leave
sufficient room for efficient competition between
the credit institutions.   This applies both to the

Table 3

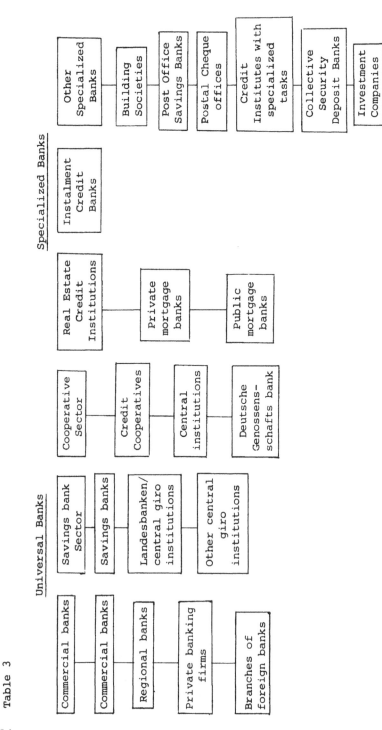

Specialized Banks

| Other Specialized Banks | Building Societies | Post Office Savings Banks | Postal Cheque offices | Credit Institutes with specialized tasks | Collective Security Deposit Banks | Investment Companies |

| Instalment Credit Banks |

| Real Estate Credit Institutions | Private mortgage banks | Public mortgage banks |

| Cooperative Sector | Credit Cooperatives | Central institutions | Deutsche Genossens- schafts bank |

Universal Banks

| Savings bank Sector | Savings banks | Landesbanken/ central giro institutions | Other central giro institutions |

| Commercial banks | Commercial banks | Regional banks | Private banking firms | Branches of foreign banks |

freedom to set up branches (promulgated in 1958),
which led to a considerable expansion in the number
of banking offices - and also, what is of greater
importance, to the absence of ceilings on interest
rates (in contrast to the famous American "Regulation Q").   In fact, the deposit rates offered by
the various credit institutions differ from each
other by about up to 1% and lending rates by as much
as about 3%.   Despite the basically competitive
orientation of the system, the Banking Law
(especially after its amendment in 1976) has succeeded in providing a satisfactory legal basis for the
central concern of any banking system, the protection of creditors and depositors.   The German system
provides this protection indirectly by seeking to
ensure that the banking system itself does not go
into bankruptcy.   It is thus similar to the practice
implicitly followed in Britain, but the opposite of
the Federal Deposit Insurance system in the US.
Yet it must be remembered that this improvement in
depositor protection became necessary because of
concrete negative experiences (the collapse of the
banking house Herstatt in 1974) and new developments
in banking activity.
    At the present time, that indirect protection
is based essentially upon three elements:

-   the provisions relating to the capital and
    reserves and the liquidity of the credit
    institutes (the socalled "liquidy princi-
    ples"), which have been supplemented since
    1976 by a sharpening-up of those concern-
    ing large loans or credits,
-   the insurance of deposits by a "deposit
    insurance fund",
-   and the establishment of a liquidity-
    syndicate bank.

    The liquidity provisions are of particular
significance for the operations of the credit
institutes, because they prescribe limits to the
way in which and the extent to which the banks can
grow.   They do so by laying down certain structural
norms, and are made up of three individual stipul-
ations (supplementing articles 10 and 11 of the
Banking Law).   Provision I restricts the total
volume of credit extended - excluding lending to
domestic public authorities - to 18 times the
capital plus reserves and retained profits; in
addition, since 1974 open foreign exchange positions
cannot exceed 30% of capital plus reserves and

retained profits (Provision Ia).   Provision II
stipulates that long-term lending should not exceed
the long-term funds available.[26]   Provision III is
a general liquidity regulation.[27]   In addition to
these provisions, no individual large loan can be
greater than 75% of the institute's own capital;
the five biggest large loans cannot exceed three
times own capital; and the upper limit for all
large loans is eight times own capital.   Hence,
while provisions I and Ia aim at restricting the
banks' ability to undertake risky business, II and
III seek to safeguard the banks' liquidity by imposing certain restrictions upon the maturity structure
of the banks' obligations.

    The insurance of deposits, on the contrary, is
directly undertaken by the "Deposit Insurance Fund"
set up in 1976; all deposits are fully insured by
it.   The degree of insurance provided is subject to
only one limitation: the individual deposits are
covered up to a sum which is 30% of the last
published net worth statement of the bank concerned.
The fund draws its resources from contributions by
the credit institutes who comprise its membership.

    While the purpose of this "deposit insurance"
is to secure the creditors of a bank against the
risk that it might become insolvent, the liquidity-
syndicate bank serves a rather different aim.   Set
up in 1974 on the initiative of the Bundesbank, its
goal is to protect from liquidity difficulties such
credit institutes as for no fault of their own
become subject to massive and unforeseen withdrawals
of deposits.   With the assent of the Credit
Committee they can draw bills on the liquidity-
syndicate bank, which are accepted by it and in turn
presented to the Bundesbank for rediscount.   The
liquidity-syndicate bank has been granted for this
purpose a rediscount quota of 500 Mill DM at the
Bundesbank.   The Bundesbank is also involved in the
syndicate along with the other banks.[28]

    In addition to these stipulations aimed at
protecting the depositors, the Banking Law also
above all imposes conditions as to the acceptability
and qualifications of the managers of credit
institutions, and the system of bank investigation
so far as it is conducted by state authorities.
This, the socalled "banking supervision", is undertaken by the Federal Banking Supervisory Office.

2. Banking Supervision
The basic function of the Federal Banking Supervisory Office (set up in 1961 with its head office

in Berlin) lies in ensuring that the provisions of
the Banking Law are adhered to.   It is charged with
the prevention of abuses in the banking system which
could endanger the security of the assets entrusted
to the banks, impair the "orderly conduct" of banking business and give rise to significant "disadvantages for the economy as a whole".   In that way the
Federal Supervisory Office is not a general com-
plaints tribunal for individual bank customers but
an institution operating in the public interest.[29]
It is an independent authority within the general
sphere of responsibility of the Federal Minister of
Finance, who is also thereby the direct superior of
its president.

        For the actual business activity of the instit-
utions from the savings banks' and cooperative
sectors, however, of basically greater importance
for supervision are the investigations which are
organised and conducted by the various associations
of credit institutions for the institutions
affiliated to them.   They take place through the
regional associations, which have conferred upon
them for the purpose a legal right of inspection.
Such inspections often provide the opportunity for
the association to give advice at the same time on
the organisation and earnings record of the institution inspected.   Finally; the Bundesbank too is
indirectly involved in bank supervision because it
is obliged to notify the Federal Supervisory Office
of any irregularities in the conduct of banking
business.

        If these supervisory regulations are compared
with those in the USA, they appear to be basically
more liberal and more strongly centralized.   The
reason is undoubtedly that the banking structure in
the USA is of a more federalized and specialized
character;   another result is that there are several
bodies with authority in this field.[30]   In Britain,
as has already been pointed out, there is no general
banking law nor is there any legal provision for
state supervision of banks.   In practice, however,
the Bank of England is the supervisory body;   its
"prudential control is generally accepted".
Legally imposed supervisory provisions exist only
for the savings banks, yet in the case of Britain
as also in that of the Federal Republic, it may be
predicted that their national regulations will in
the longer run be brought closer to those of the
other member states of the European Community.

NOTES

"Credit institutions" are defined in Art. 1 of the
Banking Law as "enterprises engaged in banking transactions, if the scope of the said transactions
requires a commercially organised business enterprise".   They thus include banks, savings banks,
mortgage banks, credit cooperatives and instalment
credit houses, but not the Bundesbank.

1.   For a description of the postwar development of the German banking system, and significant
differences between it and banking systems in other
countries, cf. Herbert Wolf, 30 Jahre Nachkriegsent-
wicklung im deutschen Bankwesen, Mainz, 1980;   for
the reference in the text, see p.111
2.   For the basic problems raised by the power
of the big banks, though concentrating upon Swiss
experience, see Ernest Kilgus, "Die Grossbanken",
Bankwirtschaftliche Forschungen, Bd. 53, Bern/
Stuttgart 1979.
3.   Cf. E. Wandel, Die Entstehung der Bank
deutscher Länder und die deutsche Währungsrenform
1948, pp. 85ff
4.   Cf. Deutsche Bundesbank, Deutsches Geld -
und Bankwesen in Zahlen 1876-1975, p. 254, and
Sonderdruck Nr. 7, p. 34
5.   Cf. Monatsberichte der Deutschen Bundesbank,
Mai 1981, Table III/25, p. 41*
6.   To a considerable extent, the actual involvement of the German banks in other companies is not
accurately reflected in the banks' balance sheets,
because it figures there only in the form of market-
able securities (shares).   The banks argue that the
possession of such securities does not imply a
participation in the companies involved, and that
they will sell them when a favourable opportunity
arises.   Yet, in so far as such packets of shares
remain in the banks' portfolios for some period of
time, they must be regarded as indicating a participation in the company involved.
7.   Cf. on this, also Ludwig Mühlhaupt,
Strukturwandlungen im westdeutschen Bankwesen,
Wiesbaden 1971, pp. 293ff
8.   The banks then exercise on behalf of their
customers the socalled "deposited-shares voting
right" (Depotstimmrecht).
9.   General public concern was aroused by the
spectacular collapse of the Herstatt Bank of
Cologne, which was forced into bankruptcy by the
foreign exchange speculations of its Luxembourg

subsidiary.

 10. Cf. Monatsberichte der Deutschen Bundesbank, various years, Table III,9

 11. Extracted from Deutsche Bundesbank, Sonder-druck No. 7, p.34

 12. See Wolf, op. cit., p.114

 13. Ibid., p.115

 14. If balance sheets totals are taken as the criterion, the Deutsche Bank is the largest of the big banks, with 40% of their total business. Then come the Dresdner Bank with 32% and the Commerzbank with 28%. The Deutsche Bank is regarded as "conservative" in its business activity, while the Dresdner has traditionally had the reputation of being a particularly active bank that has always pushed into new fields of business.

 15. Cf. Wolf, op. cit., pp. 122ff

 16. Cf. Eberhardt Ketzel, Das Kreditwesen in der Bundesrepublik Deutschland, Köln 1982, pp. 102ff

 17. Ibid., p. 99

 18. On this, see Wolf, op. cit., pp. 135ff

 19. As a rule, about 40% of the overall sum involved (saver's deposit plus the loan granted to him) must have been deposited in the savings deposit before - dependent upon the accrual of funds to the building society concerned - a loan can be granted to the borrower. The rate of interest on the loan is constant throughout the loan period, and in general amounts to 5% on the amount outstanding at any time. There is, in addition, a capital repayment whose proportion in the constant monthly repayments by the borrower rises correspondingly as the amount of the loan outstanding declines.

 20. Cf. Wolf, op. cit., pp. 142ff

 21. An extensive system for the assessment of and compensation for war burdens was set up in the Federal Republic. To take one example of its operation: house-owners whose property had escaped damage had to make payments to those whose houses had been destroyed.

 22. It is interesting that the attempt by the German subsidiary of the Chase Manhattan Bank to set up a specialized consumer credit bank on the American model ("family bank") had to be given up as a failure in 1978 after five years in business.

 23. Extracted from Ketzel, op. cit., p. 83

 24. In the USA the most significant legislation relating to the banks and comparable to the German Banking Law is the National Bank Act, supplemented by the banking laws of the individual states. There is no general banking law in Britain, but a

series of other Acts relates explicitly to banking business (e.g. the Money lenders Act of 1900/1927, the Protection of Depositors Act of 1963 and the Consumer Credit Act of 1974).

25. On the development and reform of the Banking Law, and problems that have arisen with it, see the detailed analysis of Manfred Hartmann, Ökonomische Aspekte der Reform des KWG, Stuttgart 1977

26. Long-term funds are composed of owned capital, funds obtained by the sale of one's own bonds, long-term loans taken up, 60% of the savings deposits, and 10% of the current accounts and time deposits of non-banks.

27. According to this, loans and advances, bills, dividend-bearing securities and the other assets of a credit institute should not exceed the following sum: 60% of the current accounts and time deposits of non-banks, 35% of current accounts and time deposits of credit institutes, 20% of savings deposits, 35% of the funds borrowed for less than four years, 80% of the bank's own acceptances, promissory notes and bills drawn by the bank on itself, as well as loans to customers abroad.

28. Cf. Wolf, op. cit., pp. 62ff

29. Cf. Ketzel, op. cit., pp. 125ff

30. Thus the Federal Reserve System, the State Banking Departments, the Federal Deposit Insurance Corporation and the Federal Home Loan Bank Board concurrently perform various particular control functions.

Chapter 4

THE FINANCIAL MARKETS

In general, there are strong reciprocal relationships between the nature of financial markets and
the way in which funds are employed in any particular
economy. On the one hand, financial markets accom-
odate themselves to the needs for finance and the
form in which monetary wealth is accumulated. On
the other hand, the ways in which funds are made
available and monetary wealth accumulated themselves
determine the formation of financial markets and the
structure they acquire. As a result of these close
interdependencies, which often mature over a long
period of time, a particular structure of financing
and financial markets then emerges which may differ
from those of other economies. In the Federal
Republic, the following basic characteristics are of
significance in this context: (1) by international
comparison, a large share in the borrowing done by
enterprises; (2) a high degree of financial intermediation in the flow of funds and - relatedly - the
dominance of the financing institutions; and
finally (3) a relative restriction of the financial
activities of private households to transactions
with the financing institutions (especially as
depositors with the credit institutions).
     In the following, the development of these
characteristics will first be analysed in greater
detail and briefly compared with the situation in
the USA and Britain. Then, the financial markets
will be described with respect to their extent and
their institutional characteristics, with a distinction being drawn between the capital markets
(markets for long-term funds) and the money market.

The Financial Markets

I. The Characteristics of the German Financial System

1. The New Beginning After the Currency Reform of 1948

There can scarcely be any doubt that the currency
reform of 1948 was of considerable significance for
the later, socalled German economic miracle.   This
historical judgement can be justified by pointing
out that the functioning of the goods markets is
dependent upon confidence in the value of money, and
that precisely this confidence can only be created
by maintaining the quantity of money scarce in relation to the demand for it.   The old Reichsmark
currency was no longer able to perform monetary
functions after the Second World War - and in fact
even during it - because the supply of money had
expanded in an inflationary fashion while the supply
of goods had been subjected to strict controls.
The currency reform, i.e. the conversion to a new
currency held in scarce supply, therefore became
necessary if the suppressed inflation was not to
become an open one when the controls over the supply
of goods were lifted.   Now, however valid this
judgement may be, it was not only the solution of
the inflation problem that made possible the success
of the German currency reform as a basis for the
following "economic miracle".   Equally important
was the reorganisation of the existing debt relationships within the private sector.   To use technical
terminology: not merely the currency reform of
"outside money" but also that of "inside money" (in
the sense of monetary assets in general) was of
great importance for the reconstruction of the
German economy.   This aspect of the currency reform
has often received insufficient attention; and
simultaneously, the currency reform exerted a large
influence upon the development of the particular
structure of the financial system and of financial
markets in the Federal Republic.

    That a currency reform took place at all was
essentially due to the diktat of the American
government.   On the one hand, it wanted to check
the rise in the expenses it was incurring in extending economic support to Germany and cut its occupation costs.   On the other hand, it needed a successful currency reform if the Marshall Plan was to be
carried through.   Yet the proposals as to the way
in which the reform was to be effected, and its
extent, remained for a relatively long time unclear
and subject to controversy, and the American plans
sometimes conflicted seriously with German views.[1]

The plan eventually executed was essentially the socalled CDG-Plan[2] (named after the American economists of German origin, Gerhard Colm and Ray Goldsmith, and General Clay's financial advisor, Joseph Dodge). The important advantage that it possessed over other plans was that it proposed not merely the devaluation of circulating currency and bank deposits, but also the drawing of private debts into the currency reform. The details of the reform were then finally worked out with extensive involvement of German experts[3] in the conclave at Rothwesten (20 April - 24 May) and announced to the public on the 20th of June 1948. Its main provisions were as follows: - the Reichsmark was replaced by the new currency, the Deutsche Mark; - the issue of the Deutsche Mark was restricted to 10 Mrd. DM, though the new bank notes had neither a cover provision nor could be presented for redemption; - every inhabitant could exchange their Reichsmarks for DM's in the ratio 1 : 1, up to a sum of 60 DM; firms could also obtain 60 DM per each of their employees; - current obligations (wages, rents) were converted at the ratio 1 : 1; - so far as all other obligations and demands were concerned, and hence all creditor - debtor - relationships, a writing-down was ordered in the ratio 10 : 1; for bank deposits and cash holdings, the conversion ratio was even lower, amounting to only 6.5%.

Although the public were surprised by the actual details of the reform, it had been generally expected for some time that a currency reform would sooner or later take place. This expectation had led to the hoarding of commodities, so that the new money met a sufficiently large supply of goods. The real situation of the German economy had actually experienced a considerable recovery in the years between 1945 and 1949. Production in the British and American zones had already reached 40% of the 1936 level by 1946, and in the 3rd quarter of 1948 official figures indicated that a real rate of growth of 30% had been achieved. The publication of the Marshall Plan with its announcement of raw materials shipments, and the resumption of external trade, gave rise to further optimistic expectations. But above all the German economy had a supply of human capital available, i.e. an abundant supply of well-educated workers that was being further added to by the inflow of refugees from the former Eastern territories of the Reich and from the Soviet occupation zone. To that extent, the success of the currency reform was under-pinned from the side of output. As the abolition of rationing and price controls took place quickly afterwards for most consumption and investment goods, the currency reform worked as a pump-primer for the coming "economic miracle".

Given the fact that monetary demands had been written down by the currency reform, it was also necessary to convert and revalue the balance sheets of firms. For that purpose all firms were obliged to submit in 1949 a socalled "DM Opening Balance". To the extent that an excess of liabilities over assets arose because of the writing-down of the firm's demands against the state, socalled Equalization Claims against the individual states in which the firms had their head offices were made available to them. At the stroke of a pen the central government was freed from its debts, which at the end of 1945 had amounted to 380 Mrd. Reichsmark. As a result, there was no significant public debt in the Federal Republic until well into the 60's; until the mid 70's, the state was even a net creditor in relation to the private sector. Another aspect of this revaluation, however, was also important: the currency conversion involved a marked undervaluation of the real assets of firms. The reason was that German firms possessed a productive capacity – above all because of their technical and organisational "know-how" – which was clearly valued at too low a level in the opening balances, and hence they were left with extensive "hidden reserves".

As a result, the firms' equity ratio was undervalued, and consequently yielded very high returns in the following years. This was not immediately reflected in a rise in the price of their shares on the capital market, for, firstly, the new valuation of the capital of limited liability enterprises required under the currency reform was basically not completed until 1956, and until then, therefore, a functioning market in stocks and shares simply did not exist. Secondly, the firms distributed scarcely any of their profits but accumulated them as owned capital, so that the shareholders in them received only very small dividends on their shares. But the cost of borrowing – as compared to the situation in the 60's, – was relatively high (the nominal rate of interest on loans lay 4.5% above the discount rate, on overdrafts 6%); hence it was advantageous for firms to use their own funds to finance their activities.

In addition, the capital markets initially had very little funds to offer, since existing monetary

assets had been largely devalued and, given the still
low wage-level, the mass of income-earners had only
little ability to save (until 1962, the savings
ratio of private households was well below 10%; in
1950/1, it had been only slightly more than 2%).
The limited formation of monetary assets that private
households were able to achieve was effected up to
the end of the 50's to the extent of about 75% with
banks and only to a very small amount with building
societies and insurance companies. In general, they
almost never purchased stocks and shares. As
against that, the state ran budget surpluses up to
the mid 60's, which were likewise deposited overwhelmingly with the banks, with the result that - as
noted above - the state became a net creditor of the
private sector. Given the undervaluation of the DM
against the dollar ($US 1 = DM4.20), foreign invest-
ment in German enterprises was also stimulated.

It can therefore be said that two of the three
features which still characterize the German financial markets today had already emerged after the
currency reform and during the 50's: a relative
underdevelopment of the markets in corporate issues,
and the preference of the mass of holders of monetary
assets for bank deposits, features which conferred
upon the financial institutions an important intermediary function from the very beginning. Firms
did not initially suffer from a deficiency of
capital funds, because of the considerable extent
of self-financing they could do and the elimination
of a very large part of their indebtedness by the
writing-down of the value of their debts that took
place via the currency reform. The state as well
was virtually completely freed of debt by the same
reform, and on the contrary made a positive contribution to saving activity in the economy through its
lending to firms and private households at the same
time as it ran budget surpluses. The first stages
of the reconstruction of the German economy could
consequently be financed with neither a significant
enlargement of, nor the imposition of strains upon,
the still underdeveloped capital markets.

2. Phases in the Development of the Financial System.

The subsequent development of the financial system
in the Federal Republic was marked by the increasing
significance of the intermediary activities of the
credit institutions, especially the banks. That
they achieved a dominating role as intermediaries in
the flow of funds can be attributed for one thing to
the growing ability and actual willingness of private
households to save that came about with the growth

of national income and the incomes of the broad
masses of the population.   The largest part of the
private householders' monetary assets originating
in this way was not invested in the stocks and shares
of corporations or government securities (see
table 4.1 relating to the formation of assets and
its financing, which also is of relevance to the
rest of these remarks), but placed with the banks.
At the same time, as enterprises' investment
activity grew, their need for finance began to out-
run the self-finance available to them.   Enterprises thus gradually increased the volume of
borrowed funds with which they worked, and especially that of borrowing from the banks.   As a result,
the share of firms' liabilities composed of borrowed
funds began to rise at the end of the 60's, from 60
to 65%, reaching nearly 70% during the 70's.   By
international standards, therefore, German firms
show a much higher proportion of borrowed funds in
the overall financial resources with which they
operate.
       Until the beginning of the 70's, the state
still made a positive contribution to the overall
economy's savings activity;   in fact, it remained a
net creditor of the private sector until 1974.   At
that point in time, the state began - as in other
countries too - to incur an increasing level of
indebtedness, in connection with the interruption to
economic growth that was intensified by the oil
crisis.   From then on, it appeared on the capital
markets no longer as a supplier of funds but - in
competition with private borrowers - as a demander
of them.   In this connection, the size of the
public sector deficit is determined not merely by
the particular level of economic activity that
exists but also and to a considerable extent by
structural factors, i.e. even at full utilization of
the economy's productive activity, a significant
proportion of the public sector's expenditures could
only be met by its incurring indebtedness, so long
as tax rates remained unchanged.[5]   Although efforts
were begun at the end of the 70's to diminish this
structural deficit in public sector budgets, the
political resistance to cuts in public expenditures
and/or rises in taxation are considerable, as in
other countries.   Added to that is the fact that a
weakening in investment activity and the world-wide
cyclical downswing immediately preceding and at the
beginning of the 80's led to a sharp rise in unemployment, which meant that rather narrow limits were
set to a restrictive fiscal policy for this reason

Table 4.1 Asset Formation and its Financing, By Sector of the Economy*

(in Mrd. DM)

A. Private Households

For year as whole or end-year	Current Savings	Savings Ratio	Total	Monetary Assets					
				Deposits with			Fixed-Interest Securities	Share Issues	Other debt instruments
				Banks	Building Societies	Insurance Companies			
1950	2.1	3.2%	22.0	11.8	0.5	3.7	0.3	5.5	0.9
1960	15.9	9.0%	125.4	77.2	9.2	22.2	6.2	9.9	9.0
1970	59.8	13.9%	457.1	270.0	39.6	76.3	46.8	22.8	29.1
1980	139.3	13.5%	1465.0	776.3	101.2	249.5	193.5	31.2	136.7

* Source: Deutsche Bundesbank, "Gesamtwirtschaftliche Finanzierungsrechnung", Sonderdruck No. 4.

Table 4.2   Asset Formation and its Financing, By Sector of the Economy*
(in Mrd. DM)

B. Firms, including Housing (exclusive of financial institutions)

For year as whole or end-year	Gross Investment	Current Self-financing	Monetary Assets			Liabilities		
			Total	Bank Deposits	Deposits Held Abroad	Total	Bank Borrowings	Owed abroad
1950	20.1	14.3	20.2	12.5	3.5	43.0	20.8	4.8
1960	70.0	44.7	77.5	39.1	16.8	230.5	133.1	17.6
1970	163.4	107.5	195.8	96.6	49.5	679.9	406.2	75.7
1980	312.9	210.8	572.6	278.9	162.4	1694.9	1024.8	172.5

* Source: Deutsche Bundesbank, "Gesamtwirtschaftliche Finanzierungsrechnung", Sonderdruck No. 4.

Table 4.3   Asset Formation and its Financing, By Sector of the Economy*

(in Mrd. DM)

C. The Public Sector (excluding the Bundesbank)

For year as whole or end-year	Financial Surpluses	Net Balance	Monetary Assets			Liabilities		
			Total	Bank Deposits	Deposits Held Abroad	Total	Bank Borrowings	Owed abroad
1950	2.55	-5.5	15.3	9.3	0.9	20.7	16.8	0.5
1960	9.9	45.1	100.0	59.3	6.3	53.8	35.5	6.5
1970	3.3	71.4	196.0	118.5	8.9	124.6	88.8	1.0
1980	-50.9	-197.1	285.5	173.0	9.9	482.6	311.2	31.4

* Source: Deutsche Bundesbank, "Gesamtwirtschaftliche Finanzierungsrechnung", Sonderdruck No. 4.

as well.

In discussing the development of the financial markets, therefore, it must be remembered that the state is now appearing upon them as a significant borrower. But, as is true of private firms, the largest part of the state's borrowing takes the form of bank credits. Since the credit institutions finance the public sector's indebtedness largely by the issue of bank bonds (above all mortgage bonds and local authority obligations), and hence additional monetary assets in the form of securities are created, the market for debt instruments also showed substantial growth during the 70's. On the other hand, the market for stocks and shares continued to remain relatively limited, and was only a fraction of the size of the markets for fixed interest securities (cf. in this connection the comments later in this chapter).

During its entire economic history, the Federal Republic has always had a net surplus on its dealings with abroad, a surplus which has predominantly taken the form of exchange reserves with the Bundesbank because of surpluses on the current balance and interventions in the foreign exchange market by the Bundesbank. In general, German firms as a whole have had a negative balance on capital account with abroad, even if at the end of the 70's - due also to the international interest rate differential against the Federal Republic - a tendency to a positive balance has emerged. The state, too, had also avoided contracting any significant foreign indebtedness until the mid 70's; only at that time did its net foreign liabilities show a perceptible increase in absolute terms in the face of rising public sector deficits. Yet this trend of development in the Federal Republic's balance on capital account - for the most part in equilibrium - does not mean that inflows from abroad were without any significance for German financial markets. On the contrary, they have always exerted a strong influence on those markets. Extensive movements of capital into them have been induced by, above all, expectations of changes in the exchange rate of the DM and - at the end of the 70's - international interest - rate differentials. Because of the relative narrowness of the securities' markets in the Federal Republic that has already been referred to, this has led to considerable fluctuations in the level of prices in these markets (we shall return to this matter in more detail below).

It can therefore be said that the particular

features of the German financial system : heavy
reliance on borrowed funds by firms, a high degree of
intermediation and the dominance of the financial
institutes, have developed in the period since the
currency reform.   The nature of the flow of funds
and the financial markets in the Federal Republic
are thus basically different from that in the USA
and Britain.   In these countries, the firms' debt
ratios are lower and the intermediary activity of
the financial institutions are not as pronounced,
because the private household sector is also - with
the assistance of brokers' firms - more heavily
involved in the financial markets.   By that
standard, the German financial system is also
exposed to particular risks and problems : the
relative scarcity of risk - bearing equity shares in
firms possibly diminishes their ability to innovate.
In any case, the relatively high degree of dependence on borrowed funds leads to a particular sensitivity to the level of interest rates, and so changes
in that level - and in addition, in international
interest - rate differentials - are of especial
significance for the German economy.   It is due to
the relatively high degree of financial intermediation that the risks faced by firms are largely
shared with them by the financial institutions, with
the result that there are relatively close links
between credit institutions and firms in the Federal
Republic.   Since private households hold their
monetary assets above all in the form of bank
deposits, the maintenance of a low rate of inflation
is regarded as of special importance.   The central
role played by the credit institutions in the
financial markets at the same time offers favourable
opportunities for monetary policy to effect its
function of control (which will be discussed in
detail in a later chapter).
     After the Second World War, therefore, there
prevailed in the financial system a set of conditions
that were highly favourable to the reconstruction of
the German economy, given the writing-down and even
elimination of existing public and private indebtedness.   But this has now been replaced by a completely different situation.   Both in the private and
the public sector, the volume of monetary assets and
liabilities - and thus monetary wealth - has grown
significantly more rapidly than that of real assets.
Unforeseen changes in the financial markets - and so
"monetary shocks" - have thereby acquired special
significance for the Federal Republic's economic
development.   It may well be that, because of the

particular characteristics of its financial system,
the German economy is thus more susceptible to
"monetary shocks".   That, too, explains the support
for a monetary and financial policy which is pre-
occupied with stability and stabilization of the
purchasing power of money - leaving aside the particularly negative experiences of more remote history.

II The Individual Capital Markets

1. Bank Lending

As we pointed out above, bank loans are by far the
most important financing instrument in the German
economy, from which it follows that the bank credit
market is the most important market for long-term
finance.   If the advances and loans of the banks to
private and public sector borrowers are compared to
their overall volume of business, a ratio of about
60% is shown (cf the following survey of the most
significant items in the banks' balance sheets).
This ratio has remained largely constant for a long
time, though the composition of those borrowing from
the banks has changed.   Thus, as already shown, at
present the volume of credit extended to public
authorities by the banks has grown by comparison to
that in the years before 1974, whereas the share of
private non-banks has declined - in connection with
the decline in investment and construction activity.
The significance of the credit financing of export
business has also risen, for the ability of export-
ers to compete in world markets is determined to an
increasing extent not merely by price and quality
but also by the possibility of offering medium - and
long - term credit to the purchasers.   Since export
firms often do not possess the owned funds with which
to do this, they have been forced to a corresponding
extent to borrow from the banks.[7]   (See table 4.4)
     Although the universal banks dominate the bank-
ing sector, the degree of transformation of maturities which they undertake in their financial
business is relatively small, i.e. basically, long-
term credits are financed by long-term deposits.
The latter are available to the banks essentially in
the form of savings deposits, savings certificates
and bonds.   A large part of the savings deposits
are, formally, of relative short maturity (the
socalled "legally required notice of withdrawal" for
savings deposits is only one month if more than
2000 DM are to be withdrawn), but in fact they rank
among the very long-term funds available to the banks.

Table 4.4: Significant Assets and Liabilities of the Banks
(end - 1980, in Mill. DM)+

Total Volume of Business: 2,351,260

Assets		Liabilities	
Cash holdings	7698	Deposits by Banks	601521
Deposits with the Bundesbank	63200	Deposits by non-banks	1185331
Loans to Banks	658249	Of which:	
Loans to non-banks	1542869	Current Accounts	178938
Of which:			
Advances and Loans	1365791	Time Deposits	368335
		Savings Deposits and Savings Certificates	588129
Bills discounted	53394	Bonds	413594
Securities (excluding bank bonds)	56487	Capital (inclusive of reserves shown in balance sheets)	76923
Participations	19061		

+ Source: Monatsberichte der Deutschen Bundesbank, Tabelle III 12/3.

The structural norms of the Banking Law referred to in the previous chapter also help to ensure a very high degree of maturity matching. Yet in the recent past - certainly related to the phase of high interest - rates throughout the world and the rise in public sector indebtedness - bank deposits have exhibited an increasing interest - elasticity, so that shifts from the savings deposits which yield low interest to bonds and public securities bearing higher interest have posed problems of profitability for the banks. Connected with that have been variations in the individual money aggregates, which have confronted the Bundesbank with additional problems of interpretation and control in the policy it has pursued with respect to the supply of money. (Cf in this respect the later chapter on the Bundesbank's monetary targets.)

The responsiveness of the demand for credit to changes in the interest rate, above all that by firms, which - as has already been pointed out - is relatively high in the Federal Republic, manifests itself in two directions: firstly, with respect to long-term interest rates on borrowing in general. In this context, loans for housing construction play an important role. Secondly, a feature of periods in which a fall in interest is expected or a merely temporary rise takes place is that borrowers hedge by concentrating their borrowing on short-term loans, so that at a later point, when the general level of interest has fallen, they can convert their borrowing into longer-term obligations. This type of speculative behaviour on the part of borrowers in structuring the maturity of their obligations led in the mid and final years of the 70's to an "inverse" term structure of interest rates, i.e. the interest rates on short-term funds lay perceptibly above those on long-term. The following graphical depiction of the levels reached by some selected interest rates shows this type of behaviour. (see diagram 4.2)

The level and structure of interest rates in the credit markets in the Federal Republic is, however, determined not merely by the monetary policy being pursued by the Bundesbank but also to a considerable extent by influences emenating from financial markets abroad. That this connection between domestic German interest rates and those abroad, a linkage of significance for the Federal Republic, should exist is by no means self-evident in the context of flexible (i.e. outside the EMS) exchange rates. In a regime of fixed exchange

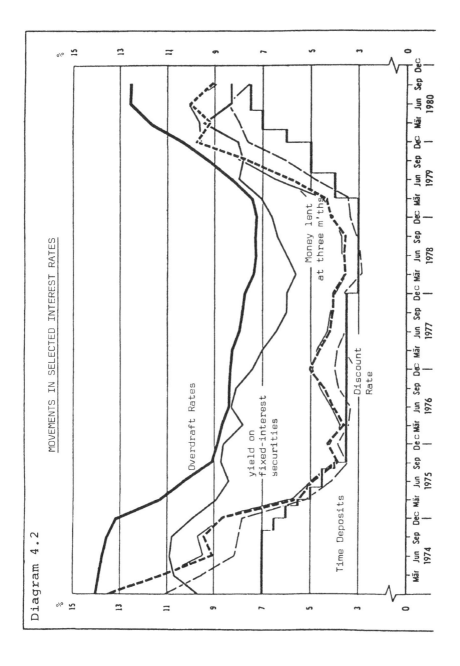

Diagram 4.2

MOVEMENTS IN SELECTED INTEREST RATES

rates, the concern is to achieve, under free international capital flows, an equalization of the level and structure of interest rates internationally with flexible exchange rates. However, it must be remembered that expectations of changes in exchange rates play an essential part in the interest rate calculations that figure in international capital flows. For example, the level of interest at home can be lower than that abroad by an amount which is dependent upon the expectation that the domestic currency will be upvalued. If, nevertheless, the level of interest rates in Germany has tended to approximate to the international - especially American - level at least temporarily (at the end of the 70's and the beginning of the 80's), that is due to two factors. For one thing, changes in exchange rates can hardly have been expected, because monetary policy in the USA took on the same (<u>i.e.</u> a restrictive) stance as in the Federal Republic.[8] For another thing, the existence of the European Monetary System (EMS) has given rise to certain imperfections in the exchange rate mechanism. For since the Bundesbank was obliged to intervene continuously on the foreign exchange markets to maintain the exchange rate parities agreed under the EMS, the exchange rate risk faced by the international investor of capital and the borrower in markets abroad was substantially reduced.

2. The Markets in Fixed-Interest Securities (Renten) and Shares

It has been pointed out above that the role played by the securities' markets in the flow of funds is essentially less in the Federal Republic than in other countries. However, because of the rise in public sector borrowing in recent years, the market for securities bearing a fixed rate of interest ("the market for fixed-interest securities and bonds") has expanded considerably, and its volume is now clearly greater than that of the share market. This development is shown in the following table 4.4 of stock exchange dealings in such securities (in Mill. DM).

The dominance of the fixed-interest securities' market becomes still more evident if, instead of stock exchange turnover, the amount of such securities in circulation is compared with that of stocks and shares (both in nominal values). Thus, at the end of 1980, the volume of domestic bonds in circulation amounted to ca. 550 Mrd. DM, while that of stocks and shares was only ca. 90 Mrd. DM.

Table 4.4

Year	Total	Domestic Issuers		Foreign Issuers	
		Fixed-Interest Securities	Stocks & Shares	Fixed-Interest Securities	Stocks & Shares
1971	26177	6287	15700	3224	964
1975	65134	30796	27466	4615	2256
1980	83177	40534	27717	9768	5154

Source: Deutsche Bundesbank

Leaving aside issues made abroad, the supply of fixed-interest securities can be divided up into three groups according to the identity of those issuing them:

    a. <u>Bonds issued by Public Authorities</u>
These public authorities include the Federal Government, the Federal Railways or the Federal Post Office, the Länder, and Local Authorities. The Federal Government is responsible for the overwhelming proportion of such issues; since the end of the 60's, it has floated them increasingly in the form of constant issues through the Bundesbank and the banking system (Federal Savings Bonds, Federal Bonds, and Financial Bonds).

    b. <u>Bank Bonds</u>
Under this collective title are included fixed-interest securities issued by private credit institutions or those of a public-law nature. Essentially, the bodies involved are mortgage banks and Landesbanken/central giro institutions, which issue mortgage bonds and local authority bonds above all. It is in this way that the issuing banks obtain a large part of the funds with which to finance the loans they have extended to the state.

    c. <u>Industrial Bonds</u>
These are issued by the larger enterprises, above all limited liability companies. As a result, the whole of the new issue is first taken up by a consortium of banks, who then place them with the public. The relative significance of industrial bonds has in the past continuously declined in volume terms. Thus, at the end of 1981 the value of such bonds on issue amounted to only ca. 4.0 Mrd. DM (as against a total value of almost 616 Mrd. DM fixed-interest securities).

Issuing activity in the fields of both public authority loans and bank bonds is subject to institutional guidance. The Central Capital Market Committee,[9] in whose meetings a representative of the Bundesbank participates by standing invitation, discusses at intervals of several weeks the situation in the securities market and makes recommendations as to the sequence in which and the time at which individual issues should be made, in order to avoid imposing excessive strain on the market. The bonds of the Federal Government, the Federal Railways and

the Federal Post Office are issued via the Federal
Loans consortium: under the leadership of the
Bundesbank, this consortium includes all the credit
institutions with substantial involvement in the
securities business.   Negotiations as to the date
of issue, its size and the conditions attached to it
are then negotiated in the socalled Smaller Committee
of the Federal Loans consortium.   The socalled "loan
timetable", which fixes for the consortium the time
at which the public bonds are to be placed in the
securities markets, is drawn up by the Economic
Policy Council (Konjunkturrat der Öffentlichen Hand).
The latter is under the leadership of the Federal
Finance Ministry, and is composed of representatives
of the Federal Government, the Länder and the local
authorities, with the Bundesbank regularly participating in its deliberations.
    It is in line with the particular nature of the
flow of funds in the Federal Republic that, as
universal banks, the credit institutions are not
merely the most significant emitters of fixed-
interest securities (in the form of bank bonds) but
also compose the most significant component of the
demand for them.   Thus at the end of 1981 the banks
held in their own possession about two-fifths of the
total volume of bonds in circulation (cf the
following table 4.5), or a significantly larger
volume than private persons, who owned only about
150 Mrd. DM of the more than 600 Mrd. DM of such
bonds.   Insurance companies and private enterprises,
too, have purchased fixed interest securities.   That
private enterprises have done so in considerable
volume is to be attributed above all to the relatively high rate of return on public sector bonds in
past years, which have exceeded those on other forms
of investment and especially often those on real
investments as well.   The following table summar-
ises the total volume of bonds in circulation and
their distribution among various groups of holders.
    Most of the fixed interest securities dealt in
within the Federal Republic have - as also in other
countries - the legal form of socalled bearer bonds,
i.e. those actually in possession of them are
legitimately entitled to the interest etc. on them.
By virtue of this particular legal form, dealings
in them on the eight German stock exchanges are
considerably facilitated;   for, in contrast to
assigned bonds ("Order und Rektapapieren"), they do
not bear the name of the respective creditor.   In
general, the bonds acquired by purchasers are not
handed over to them but deposited in the centralized

Table 4.5 : Volume of Domestic Bonds in Circulation and Distribution of Holdings (Nominal Values in Milliard DM, as at end-1981)

Volume in Circulation		Distribution of Holdings	
Bank bonds	484.4	Domestic Banks	240.9
of which:		Deutsche Bundesbank	4.3
Mortgage Bonds	110.7	Private Persons	151.7
Local Authority Bonds	240.9	Insurance Companies	70.2
Bonds of institution with specialised functions	32.1	Social Insurance Fund	13.7
Other	100.7	Business Firms	26.3
Public Authorities' Bonds	127.8	Foreigners	22.3
Industrial Bonds	4.0	Others not accounted for by the above categories	86.4
Total	615.8	Total	615.8

Source: Volume in Circulation: Statist. Beihafte to the Monatsberichte der Deutschen Bundesbank, Reihe 2, Wertpapierstatistik, Tab. 5a.; Distribution of Holdings: Monatsberichte der Deutschen Bundesbank, Depoterhebung für 1981.

collective depositories of the banking system.

Developments in the bond markets are significantly influenced by the current level of economic activity and the policy being pursued by the Bundesbank. When economic activity is rising sharply and the Bundesbank is conducting a restrictive policy, credit institutions frequently dispose of the securities they have purchased - despite the rise in interest rates that is occurring -so as to avoid the necessity of restricting their loans and advances to their private customers. For the same reason, they expand the volume of bonds (socalled Other Bonds, whose issue is not linked to any particular form of lending and investment business) they offer to their depositors, in order to acquire additional liquidity, for bonds are not subject to the minimum reserve obligations. At times of weakening economic activity, on the other hand, when the Bundesbank is making additional liquidity available to them, the credit institutes attempt to make up for the decline in the private demand for credit by purchasing more securities.

Because of the markedly anti-cyclical character of their savings activity, private households pursue a type of investment behaviour which is similar to that of the credit institutions. In cyclical downswings, they generally raise their savings for motives of caution, while they lower them in boom conditions. While this behaviour is typical of the situation in the Federal Republic, it is clearly the opposite of that which prevails in other countries, above all in the USA. The basic explanation of it lies in the fact that private households have a lower level of indebtedness in the Federal Republic, so that they can increase their savings and/or reduce their expenditures even when the level of income is declining. This behaviour has weakened somewhat in the most recent past, however, because in the recession there has taken place not merely a decline in the growth of real income but even an absolute reduction, and the private households' indebtedness (contracted via consumer and mortgage borrowing) has risen. Yet - linked with a perceptible increase of interest - sensitivity - their basic willingness to purchase fixed interest securities has simultaneously risen. To that extent, a larger share of the overall volume of fixed - interest securities in circulation will certainly be able to be placed with private households in the future.

That the private households, given that their

investments are determined by precautionary motives,
exert a stronger demand for fixed-interest securities
than for shares, is due above all to the relative
stability of the prices of such securities. The
Bundesbank contributes to this stability by intervening on the securities' market to moderate price
fluctuations, though these socalled "price support
operations" must not be confused with the employment
of the policy instrument of open market operations.

Apart from the aversion to risk exhibited by
the investment behaviour of most private households
in the Federal Republic, the basic reasons for
what - measured in terms of the size of the German
economy - is a relatively small market in stocks and
shares have already been given : the extent to which
German firms rely upon borrowed funds and the
dominant intermediary role played by the credit
institutions in the flow of funds. Yet, since their
lack of own funds increasingly poses serious problems
of financing for firms, the attempt has continuously
been made - by the state taking the initiative as
well - to interest more small savers in acquiring
stocks and shares. Thus a part of the Federal
Government's holdings in various enterprises were
privatized by the issue of socalled "Volksaktien"
(i.e. low-denomination shares for small savers) :
the undertakings involved were Preussag (1959), the
Volkswagen works (1961) and Veba (1965). By making
these issues on favourable terms, the Government did
at first succeed in placing these Volksaktien among
broad groups of savers, but after a few years the
ownership of these shares became concentrated in the
hands of the financial institutions and large-scale
investors. At the present time, particular measures
by the state are under consideration to promote
saving via the purchase of shares, similar to those
seeking to encourage saving through building
societies.

In addition to stocks and shares, by far the
most significant titles to ownership handled by the
German stock exchanges, the latter also deal in
special types of participation; shares in mining
companies formed in the early nineteenth century,
the socalled Kuxe, and income notes (Gewinnscheine),
which in general establish the right to a share in
profits. There are also intermediate forms which
embody an option to take up a participation of a
claim on profits: there are the convertible bonds
or option loans, which give the lender the right to
subscribe for shares at a fixed price. In
addition, the stock exchanges deal in participating

debentures, which carry fixed interest plus a share of profits and whose yield therefore varies predominantly with respect to the profit distribution made by the limited liability company issuing the debenture.11

As in the case of fixed-interest securities, dealings in shares and other participation titles take place on the eight regional stock exchanges in Berlin, Bremen, Düsseldorf, Frankfurt, Hamburg, Hanover, Munich and Stuttgart.12   Until the outbreak of the Second World War, Berlin was the leading banking and stock exchange centre, but today it is Frankfurt, Düsseldorf, Munich and Hamburg which are the leaders.   Munich plays a significant role above all in bond dealings.   Transactions on the stock exchanges are - in contrast to the Anglo-Saxon brokerage system - conducted by the credit institutes which are active as universal banks.   The only use made of brokers is in the finalisation of the deal: they establish the prices of the shares concerned, which form the basis for the settlement statement relating to the commissions carried out by the credit institutions.   Such brokers are pledged to conduct their business impartially and are appointed by the respective Land Governments within whose area of authority the stock exchange is located.   Their role is to offer to the public not directly involved in stock exchange dealings the guarantee that they will not be overreached by the credit institutions acting on their behalf.   In addition to the strictly organised stock exchanges, socalled "unofficial dealings" have developed, in which a distinction is drawn between "requested unofficial dealings" and "over-the-counter telephone dealings".   In the former, which takes place during stock exchange business hours and on its premises, unofficial brokers act as intermediaries between the credit institutions.13

III The Money Market

In the Federal Republic, the term "money markets" refers basically to the aggregate dealings in credit balances at the central bank between credit institutions, as well as those in money market paper between the credit institutions and the Bundesbank. The German concept thus differs not merely from that customarily employed in macroeconomic theory, which includes both transactions in outside-money and those in inside-money.   It is also different from the

similar concepts used in the credit systems of other
countries, in which non-banks too are active in the
money market.   In positive terms, in the Federal
Republic, only credit institutions deal with one
another and with the Bundesbank in the "money
market";   and the dealings relate to short-term
liabilities (deposits and money market paper) of the
Bundesbank.[14]   The money market in its Federal
Republic image thus corresponds most closely to the
"federal funds market" in the USA and the "traditional short-term money market" in Britain.

   To the extent that the credit institutions deal
with each other on the money market, they do so
predominantly to adjust their individual liquidity
positions, with the aim of having available to them
a sufficient quantity of central bank liabilities
to fulfill the reserve obligations currently in
force.   In this context, the concept of central
bank liabilities must be distinguished from that of
the quantity of central bank money, the target
variable employed by the Bundesbank.   The quantity
of central bank money is a fictitious magnitude,
composed of currency in circulation and the minimum
reserve deposits held by the credit institutions in
proportion to their domestic liabilities.   The
latter in turn is also a fictitious value: it is
calculated on the basis of the constant average
reserve ratios in force in January 1974.   (A more
detailed analysis of the concept of central bank
money is contained in Chapter 6).   In contrast,
the central bank liabilities dealt with in the money
market are the actually-existing assets of the credit
institutions with the Bundesbank (hence with the
individual Land central banks):   their current (non-
fictitious) minimum reserve ratios at actual (not
constant historical) ratios plus their "net free
reserves".

   Since excess reserves yield no return, they are
held to a bare minimum (in general they amount to no
more than 1% of the obligatory minimum reserve
deposits).   Hence the main aim of the transactions
in central bank liabilities in the interbank money
market is the balancing-out of any contingent
deficits and surpluses with respect to the minimum
reserve obligations of individual credit institutions.   Such discrepancies emerge because the
individual credit institutions can only imperfectly
predict the behaviour of their deposits;   hence
they cannot know in advance precisely what will be
the level of minimum reserve deposits they must hold
with the Bundesbank, given that the latter obligation

is determined by the level of their deposits on definite reference dates. Since they will at the same time seek to avoid the accumulation of excess reserves, they set at as low a level as possible the volume of central bank liabilities they hold and offer their excess reserves on the money market to those banks which foresee an inability to meet precisely their minimum reserve obligations.

The period to maturity involved in dealings between the credit institutions in the money market ranges from one day up to (a maximum of) one year. For that reason, the overall market can be split up into a number of partial markets: those for money for one day, one month, three months, six months and twelve months.[15] While the money market does not possess the institutional form of an Official Exchange, it is characterized by fixed practices ("usage"). In most cases, dealings are transacted by the money dealers of the banks either by telephone or telex; security for the sums borrowed is basically not asked for or offered, since there is no doubt as to the solvency of the banks participating in money market dealings. It is the bank looking for funds that as a rule contacts those with funds to lend and an agreement between them as to the amount of any conditions upon the loan then follows.[16]

The conduct of the Bundesbank is of decisive importance for the money market, since it is the Bundesbank which basically controls the conditions upon which the credit institutions can acquire additional central bank assets on the money market. If the credit institutions are in general going to be able to fulfill their minimum reserve requirements, naturally the availability of central bank assets in sufficient quantity is a fundamental presupposition. But at the same time the Bundesbank is thereby able to set the conditions on which the credit institutions can acquire additional central bank money, i.e. it can enforce in the money market its views as to the level of interest rates in that market and thereby influence the level and structure of other rates as well. The influence it exerts on interest rates in the money market is thus also an important starting point for its control over the supply of money.

The Bundesbank can react with a series of measures (instruments) to changes in the demand for central bank money that arise from the business operations of the credit institutions, and thus pursue its interest-rate and money-supply goals by

inducing a tightening or easing of the money market.
The "coarse tuning" of the supply of central bank
money takes place through the utilization of the
usual range of monthly policy instruments (above all,
policy with respect to the discount and Lombard
rates, and Open Market policy, all of which are dealt
with in the following chapter). In addition, however, the Bundesbank has several short-term instruments with which it is able to "fine tune" the money
market. Typical of such instruments are:[17]

- transactions in money market paper,
- sale and repurchase agreements involving
  foreign exchange and foreign exchange swap
  transactions,
- operations with the deposits of public
  authorities.

Money market paper is essentially composed of
Treasury Bills, non-interest-bearing Treasury Bonds
("U-Schätze"), and prime acceptances (Privatdis-
konten). They originate either to cover a short-
term need for credit on the part of their issuers, as
a rule the Federal Government; in this case they
are known as "financing paper". Or they may be
issued solely to facilitate the monetary policy aims
of the Bundesbank, in which case they are termed
"mobilization" or "liquidity paper". The proceeds
from their sale are immobilized in the Bundesbank,
which also is responsible for the payment of interest
upon them. A proportion of money market paper bears
a socalled "assurance of rediscount" by the Bundesbank: it stands ready to buy back this paper at any
time - and so prior to its maturity date as well -
for deposits at the central bank. Hence this paper
is, for the credit institutions, virtually the same
thing as deposits with the central bank and hence is
included in their "free liquid reserves".[18] To
exercise influence on the money market, the Bundesbank varies the range between the rates at which it
issues and repurchases this paper.
     Sale and repurchase agreements relating to
bills and securities are a relatively new aspect of
the Bundesbank's operations: they were introduced
for the former in 1973 and for securities in 1979.
Their purpose is to make available, on a short-term
basis, deposits with the central bank and because of
the limited time to which they relate they form a
reversible part of the control of the money supply.
The Bundesbank can influence the credit institutions
relatively "more noiselessly" by varying the interest

rate on sale and repurchase agreements with them
than by changing the "leading rates", the discount
and Lombard rates.   Thus, for example, a rise in
money market rates because of a deficiency in
central bank deposits can often be avoided by making
such deposits available with a simultaneous cut in
the rates prevailing in sale and repurchase agreements.[20]

It is only since 1979 that the Bundesbank has
also effected foreign exchange sale and repurchase
agreements with domestic credit institutions.   In
contrast to similar dealings in bills and securities,
the purpose of those in foreign exchange is to
extract liquidity from the money market.   To this
end, the Bundesbank transfers to the credit institutions mainly claims on its US dollar-foreign assets,
for which the credit institutions pay by drawing on
their deposits at the central bank.   In this way
the volume of liquidity in the money market is
diminished and interest rates in that market tend to
rise.[21]   (The methods employed by the Bundesbank in
its operations in the foreign exchange market will
be outlined in the section of the following chapter
dealing with the range of instruments possessed by
the Bundesbank in the field of foreign payments).

The policy followed with respect to the deposits
of public funds (according to section 17 of the
Bundesbank Law) is based on the obligation of the
Federal Goverment, its Special Funds and the Länder
to deposit their liquid funds basically in accounts
at the Bundesbank, and these accounts moreover bear
no interest.   The Bundesbank may then permit these
authorities to place a portion of their deposits
with the credit institutions, whose assets at the
central bank thereby expand and the money market is
rendered more liquid.   This "deposit policy" thus
has precisely the same effect on the money market
as the sale and repurchase agreements relating to
securities.

In general, therefore, the Bundesbank has
available to it a series of quite effective
instruments which can be applied in appropriate
intensity and through which it is able to exert a
high degree of influence over the development of
interest rates in the money market.   This ability
to exercise control rests at basis on the fact that
no credit institution will pay more for funds in the
market for one-day funds than it has to at the
Bundesbank, while conversely no bank would lend
central bank deposits on the money market at an
interest rate lower than that at which it could also

obtain by dealings with the Bundesbank. Certainly,
in the formation of money market interest rates for
longer periods there is absent the tight restriction
imposed by the minimum reserve period, but in this
context the discount rate will on most occasions
constitute the lower limit for interest rates. That
is true for so long as the credit institutions can
reduce their rediscount obligations to the Bundesbank
by taking up monthly and three-monthly money. Above
that lower limit, money market interest rates for
longer periods will orientate themselves for the most
part to that on one-day money.22

NOTES

1. In this connection, emphasis should be
given to the "Hamburg Plan" hammered out by the
Special Agency "Money and Credit" of the Bizonal
Economic Council without knowledge of the CDG Plan.
But other proposals had already been put forward,
e.g. the "Binder Plan", formulated by Paul Binder
in 1945 and approved by a Commission composed of
government and banking representatives from
Württemberg.
2. The CDG Plan was supplemented with extensive
appendices, which presented a wide-ranging and
comprehensive analysis of Germany's financial structure directly after the Second World War. To a
considerable extent, this analysis was composed by
those working closely with Colm and Goldsmith,
including Lloyd Metzler, Horst Mendershausen, Robert
Eisenberg, Jerome Jacobson and Gerald Matchett. On
the CDG Plan, see Hans Möller, Zur Vorgeschichte der
Deutschen Mark, Veröffentlichungen der List-
Gesellschaft, Bd. 22, pp. 214ff (Basel/Tübingen
1961); and Heinz Sauermann, "Der amerikanische Plan
fur die deutsche Währungsreform", in HdSW, 8th ed.,
Bd. 11, the article on "Währungsreformen".
3. The Germans participating in the Rothwesten
Conclave were Karl Bernard, Wolfgang Budczies, Walter
Dudek, Heinrich Hartlieb, Erwin Hielscher, Hans
Möller, Otto Pfleiderer, Edward Wolf and Victor Wrede.
4. For an extensive analysis of the history of
the currency reform, see Eckhard Wandel, Die Entstehung der Bank deutscher Länder und die deutsche
Währungsreform von 1948
5. With the aid of its own budget concept, the
socalled "budget with neutral effect upon the level
of economic activity", the Sachverständigenrat zur
Begutachtung der gesamtwirtschaftlichen Entwicklung
presents annually a detailed analysis of the effects

of public authorities' budgetary actions in the
Federal Republic. The Sachverständigenrat was set
up by law and publishes an annual report on the
economic situation in the Federal Republic. The
fundamental features of its "neutral budget" concept
(or rather, the most up-to-date version of it) are
described in its Annual Report for 1979, pars. 229ff

6. At the end of 1980, the number of registered
unemployed in the Federal Republic was about 1.1
million; by the end of 1982, it had risen to 2.5
million.

7. In the financing of exports by the banking
system in the Federal Republic, two credit institutes
with special functions are also involved: the
consortium of the Export Credit Company (Ausführk-
redit-Gesellschaft) (AKA), in which the Deutsche
Bank plays the leading role; and the Kreditanstalt
für Wiederaufbau. The AKA is a purely private
financial institution, and specializes wholly upon
the financing of export business. For this purpose,
it has available to it three quotas (A, B and C) to
the amount of which it can rediscount bills at the
Bundesbank. The medium and long-term export
finance credits granted via the AKA do not appear
in the Bundesbank statistics among the medium and
long-term credits to the banks but as short-term
lending on bills. See Ludwig Mühlhaupt, Strukturwandlungen im westdeutschen Bankwesen, pp. 189 ff

8. In this connection, see Sachverständigenrat
zur Begutachtung der gesamtwirtschaftlichen
Entwicklung, Jahresgutachten 1980, pars. 200, 201

9. The Central Capital Market Committee was
set up in 1957. All issuing groups (with the
exception of the public authorities) belong to it,
giving it a membership of eleven. Since 1968, the
Committee has also had a Subcommittee, consisting of
six members, which administers the system of voluntary self-control observed by foreign borrowers with
respect to their DM issues.

10. Extracted from Sonderdruck der Deutschen
Bundesbank, No. 7, p. 36

11. Cf. Eberhart Ketzel, Das Kreditwesen in der
Bundesrepublik Deutschland, p. 138

12. As establishments of the relevant Chambers
of Industry and Trade, the stock exchanges in Berlin,
Frankfurt and Hamburg are public-law corporations;
the others are conducted under civil law by socalled
Stock Exchange Associations.

13. Cf. Ketzel, op. cit., p. 133

14. Certainly there are other definitions of
what constitutes the money market in the Federal

Republic.   Thus, a very broad definition of it sees it as the market for all short-term credit trans- actions.   But this definition seems inappropriate, both because it is less precise than, and because it differs from, that customarily employed when discus- sing the German credit system.   In this context, see also Wolfgang Gebauer, "Geldmarkt", in Handbuch der Wirtschaftswissenschaften, new ed., Article IX in the section "Geldtheorie und Geldpolitik", pp 476ff

15.   By "daily money" is understood loans which must be repaid by noon of the following day.   "One- day money" can be recalled at a day's notice; "daily money until further notice" is loaned without any fixed term.   "Ultimo money" is deposits at the central bank dealt in on the money market, with maturities stretching beyond the end of the month or year.

16.   Cf. Gebauer, loc. cit., p. 480

17.   Ibid., p. 481

18.   The Bundesbank defines "free liquid reser- ves" as the sum of: excess reserves;   money market paper with assurance of rediscount;   and unutilised rediscount quotas.   Before the concept of "central bank money" took on the role as the intermediate target of the Bundesbank in 1974, this function was filled by free liquid reserves.

19.   For bills, the sale and repurchase agree- ment normally covers a period of 10 to 20 days; for securities, 30 days.

20.   Cf. Gebauer, op. cit., 483

21.   Ibid., p. 483ff

22.   Ibid., p. 485

Chapter 5

THE INSTRUMENTS OF MONETARY POLICY

As the features of the US banking system provided
the example by relation to which the organisational
structure and constitution of the Bundesbank were
determined, so also for the range and type of
monetary instruments available to the Bundesbank.
Thus the instruments possessed by it are largely the
same as those of the Federal Reserve System, even if
their design may differ in some details.   There
does exist, however, a basic difference in the way
in which the instruments are used, or better in the
emphasis placed upon individual instruments.   This
is due above all to the special features of the way
in which central bank money originates in the
Federal Republic, viz. the dominance of the external
and financing components of the money supply as
compared to the fiscal component.   For in contrast
not merely to the USA but to Britain as well,
central bank money has originated in the Federal
Republic above all through the growth of foreign
exchange reserves and the indebtedness of the banks
with the Bundesbank.   In the USA and Britain on the
other hand, the indebtedness of the state to the
central bank has been of far greater significance
for the creation of "high-powered money".   Consequently, for the Bundesbank the instruments relating
to foreign trade and payments and sources of credit,
but also minimum reserve policy, have been of
special significance, while in the USA open market
operations have been of more importance.
      Another important distinction between the
regulations and monetary policy behaviour of the
Bundesbank and those of central banks in other
countries may consist in the fact that the operation
of the instruments of monetary policy in the Federal
Republic appears to have been basically much more
market-orientated than in those other countries.

That may be attributed, firstly, to the influence of external economic conditions upon the framework within which monetary policy is conducted in the Federal Republic. But, secondly, it may also be traced to the general consensus that prevails as to the efficiency of a freely-operating market. To take but one example : in contrast to the USA, there has been no regulation of interest rates since the mid - 60's. Finally, the existence of the universal banking system means that there is a marked absence of special regulations and controls such as those relating to particular groups of credit institutions whose business is confined to certain areas.

In what follows, the nature and design of the Bundesbank's individual instruments will first be described. In this context, a distinction will be drawn between instruments which seek to control the creation of central bank money (credit and external instruments) and those which influence the use made of central bank money that has already come into existence (open market and minimum reserve policy). Then the use of these instruments that can be observed in the past will be discussed with respect to what this says about the relative significance that has been attached to each of them, and the employment of them together in a few typical problem situations will be illustrated.

I The Individual Instruments

1. Discount Policy

The term "discount policy" refers - as in other countries - to the employment of instruments which influence and/or control the volume of lending by the Bundesbank to the credit institutions. Lending to them takes place either through the purchase of bills (rediscount credit) or lending against the pledge of securities (Lombard credit). The aim of lending policy is to control the circulation of money and the volume of lending; in conducting this policy, the Bundesbank operates through interest rates and quantitative restrictions upon this type of discount business. But it can influence only indirectly whether the credit institutions avail themselves either of discount or of Lombard credit, e.g. by raising their minimum reserve obligations.

According to section 19 of the Bundesbank Law, the Bundesbank has the right to purchase and to sell trade bills originating from the credit institutions, but also Treasury Bills issued by the public author-

ities, at discount rates set by itself, in so far as
these bills fulfill certain minimum requirements.
Thus, the bills should bear three names recognized as
solvent; they must mature within three months of
purchase; and they must be socalled "good" trade
bills. The volume in which the Bundesbank purchases
bills of this type is determined by the rediscount
quotas established for each individual credit institution.[1] First the overall volume of quotas is set
by the Bundesbank, and then distributed among the
individual institutions. To do so, it applies to
the socalled standard quota a multiplier based upon
the overall volume. The standard quota of the
individual institution is in turn set by relation to
its capital plus reserves and retained profits and
its share in the short-term credit business with non-
banks.[2] At the end of 1981, the overall level of
rediscount quotas amounted to 46.5 Mrd. DM. In the
past, this figure has on several occasions been
raised or lowered, depending upon the requirements
of monetary policy. Thus, in an attempt to check
the inflow of funds from abroad, it was temporarily
cut by the amount by which particular types of
obligations to foreigners were growing. In
1973/73, when the Bundesbank was conducting a rigor-
ously restrictive policy, the rediscount quotas
could not be used to their full extent but only up
to a certain percentage.

The usage made of the rediscount quotas by the
credit institutions depends, of course, upon the
level of the discount rate, or more precisely its
level relative to that of interest rates in the
money market. In setting its discount rate, the
Bundesbank has no legal maximum or minimum level to
take into account; since the Bundesbank Law came
into effect, the discount rate has moved within the
range from $2\frac{3}{4}\%$ (1959) to $7\frac{1}{2}\%$ (1970, 1980). This
rate is also applied to the cash advances made to
the public authorities within the framework of the
legally laid-down ceilings on such advances. Like
discount policy in general, changes in the discount
rate constitute above all "signals" of basic changes
in the direction of monetary policy. Hence the
beginning of an expansive policy is frequently introduced by a cut in the discount rate, followed later
by further easing in policy. Yet it is not this
single function alone which is served by discount
policy, even though at an earlier time the public
may have gained something of an impression that it
was, in view of the dominance of external and
minimum reserve instruments in the operations of the

Bundesbank. It is above all in conjunction with the employment of other instruments (especially minimum reserve ratios) that discount policy has been of significance, and that significance is bound to increase in the long-run if the external components of the money supply decline in relative weight.

Discount policy is supplemented by the instrument of Lombard policy. Under Section 19 of the Bundesbank Law, the Bundesbank can extend loans at interest to the credit institutes against their pledging ("Lombarding") of certain types of securities and bonds. The securities eligible for this purpose are more precisely defined in the socalled "eligible security list." It includes bills eligible for rediscount at the Bundesbank, non-interest-bearing Treasury Bills, bonds and debt instruments of the state, equalization claims, and debt items explicitly defined as eligible by the Bundesbank. The maximum that can be lent varies as between different types of security, between 75% and 90% of the current market or face value.[3]

The Lombard rate, i.e. the interest rate which the Bundesbank charges on Lombard loans, is always above the discount rate, and indeed by between 1% and 3%. It is thus made clear that Lombard credit is intended only as a supplement to discount borrowing; in the view of the Bundesbank, its purpose is merely to cover the "temporary shortage of liquidity" experienced by a credit institution. As a result, if the Bundesbank gains the impression that Lombard loans are being taken up in considerable volume and for longer periods of time, it will restrict or even withdraw Lombard facilities from the credit institution concerned.[4]

From the viewpoint of the credit institutions themselves, there are in general two reasons why, leaving aside the possibility that they are facing an extreme scarcity of central bank money, they might take up the more expensive Lombard loans rather than discount loans. In the first place, Lombard borrowing will be preferred when there is only little scope for further borrowing by discount, but the situation in the domestic or above all in the international money market offers rewarding prospects for lending out the liquidity obtained by Lombarding. In the second place, Lombard borrowing will be preferred to bill rediscounting when it is a question of meeting very short-term needs for liquidity. The reason is that in rediscounting bills for the credit institutions, the Bundesbank charges interest for at least five days. Hence,

if the need for liquidity relates to a shorter
period of time than that, discount credit can be
(despite the lower discount rate) more expensive
than Lombard credit, interest upon which is reckoned
only for the actual length of time for which the
loan is outstanding.[5]

2. Instruments Relating to Foreign Transactions
It has already been pointed out several times above
that the external position has always been of
especial significance for the policy followed by the
Bundesbank. Again, reference has been made to the
fact that in the past the largest part of the supply
of central bank money in the Federal Republic has
originated from the external source. Yet the
instruments whose employment is orientated exclusively or even dominantly towards foreign transactions
are not very numerous. This is because all
monetary policy instruments, even if they are at
first employed and/or become effective in domestic
financial markets, also to a considerable effect
have repercussions on the external situation, with
adjustments taking place in the foreign exchange
market as well. For example, a rise in interest
rates in the domestic money market can lead to
inflows of funds from abroad, and thereby bring about
an appreciation in the DM's exchange rate. Conversely, a reduction in minimum reserve obligations can
stimulate capital exports and/or lead to a decline
in the DM's exchange rate. For that reason,
instruments which are exclusively orientated towards
foreign transactions have more of the function of
supplementing the Bundesbank's other monetary policy
instruments. The Bundesbank itself declares that
it is the function of these instruments to "limit the
disturbances to monetary policy" which originate in
the foreign exchange markets.[6]
     To be emphasised in this context is first of all
the foreign exchange swap policy of the Bundesbank,
which is the same as that practiced by other
countries. In a swap transaction, the Bundesbank
purchases (sells) foreign exchange spot and simultaneously sells (purchases) it forward. The swap
rate is then defined as the difference between forward and spot rates as a proportion of the spot rate.[7]
A positive differential between forward and spot
rates is termed a "forward premium" (Report), a
negative differential a "forward discount" (Deport).
By raising the forward premium, or by causing it to
emerge, the Bundesbank can induce outflows of funds;
conversely, by the creation or raising of the forward

discount, it can stimulate inflows of funds. Swap transactions were undertaken by the Bundesbank for the first time in 1958. At that time its primary aim was to promote outflows of funds, in order to encourage the credit institutions to build up a stock of short-term assets abroad. On later occasions, since the end of the 60's, its purpose has been predominantly the support of the dollar parity agreed under the Bretton Woods system, i.e. it sought to ward off monetary inflows. After the floating of the DM in 1973, too, swap transactions were undertaken to bring about a "controlled" float. During the 70's, however, swap policy became to an ever increasing extent an instrument for influencing developments in the domestic money market.

Since 1979, it has been supplemented by socalled foreign exchange sale and repurchase transactions, the purpose of which is to skim off liquidity from the money market. In such transactions, the Bundesbank temporarily transfers its foreign assets denominated in US dollars to the credit institutions, who earn interest upon them. Since the transaction means a decline in the volume of liquid funds available to the money market, a rise in interest rates can thereby be brought about. Transactions of this type therefore aid above all the fine steering of the domestic money market and can be employed with a high degree of flexibility.

In addition to these "market" instruments for exerting influence upon the foreign exchange markets, various administrative measures are available for the same purpose, though these fall within the authority of the Federal Government and not the Bundesbank. The means to restrict international capital transactions are laid down in the Foreign Trade and Payments Law (Aussenwirtschsftsgesetz) (AWG). According to section 23 of the AWG, restrictions can be imposed upon capital imports if they might intensify domestic inflationary developments or if equilibrium in the balance of payments (in the sense of net foreign exchange movements) is to be secured. Such restrictions may involve either the imposition of the obligation to obtain a permit for capital imports or even the complete banning of them. Similarly, the payment of interest on foreign-owned deposits with German banks can be made subject to permission to do so, or prohibited outright. The Federal Government repeatedly imposed restrictions upon capital imports under section 23 of the AWG when, at the beginning of the 70's, the inflow of dollars into the Federal Republic sharply rose in connection with the crisis

in the international system of fixed exchange rates.
    The AWG was supplemented - likewise in 1971 -
by the socalled "Bank Deposit Obligation" (Bardepotpflicht).   The purpose of the latter was to set
limits to capital imports which stemmed from borrowing abroad by domestic residents.   Its effect was
to indirectly raise the interest costs associated
with such borrowing by requiring the domestic
residents to hold as non-interest-bearing deposits
with the Bundesbank ("cash deposit") a part of the
funds borrowed abroad.   In 1973 a maximum level of
100% was placed upon the cash deposit, and deposits
to meet minimum reserve obligations were explicitly
excluded from the scheme.   The cash deposit obligation has up till now been operated only in the
years 1972 to 1974.

II Instruments to Control the Use Made of Central
Bank Money

1. Open Market Operations

The classification of open market operations among
the possibilities open to the Bundesbank to control
the use made of central bank money already in
existence is somewhat problematical.   Against doing
so is the fact that the purchase of securities on
the "open market" by the central bank increases the
supply of central bank money.   If the central bank
uses state debt titles as the intervention paper, it
therefore acquires liabilities of the state in
exchange for its own liabilities (in the form of
central bank money).   This procedure might therefore
be described as the usual form taken by the "fiscal
component" of the money supply.   Here, therefore,
we shall deviate from the classification customary
in the analysis of the creation of central bank money
in other countries, for the aim of open market policy
and the way in which it is conducted show basic
differences from that in e.g. the USA and Britain.
    The Bundesbank does not conduct open market
operations for the purpose of controlling the fiscal
components of the supply of central bank money, for
it is explicitly prohibited from "direct intervention
in the capital market with the aim of financing the
public authorities' need for credit."[8]   In the
Federal Republic, the provision that the Bundesbank
can buy or sell only "on the open market" implies
that it cannot directly take up debt titles from
those issuing them, especially the state.   To that
extent, open market purchases by the Bundesbank

cannot be regarded as an instrument for making
central bank money available in the longer term, in
the sense of the fiscal components of the money
supply.   The reasons for this broad prohibition are
to be found in the historical experiences of Germany
that have been frequently referred to above, experiences which have given rise to basic objections
against this form of central bank money creation.

These considerations therefore also explain the
type of open market operations undertaken by the
Bundesbank, for they are conducted predominantly in
money market papers with the aim of exerting short-
term influence upon the situation in the money
market.[9]   Although long-term debt instruments may
be used in addition to such money market paper as
the Treasury Bills and Treasury Bonds of the Federal
Government, its Special Funds and the Länder, the
Bundesbank has in the past intervened with such long-
term instruments only relatively seldom.   (While
"price support" operations in public loans are
carried out by the Bundesbank, these cannot be
included in open market operations because of their
nature and their aim).   There is also a more basic
reason for this : the Bundesbank has never had in
its possession for any length of time a substantial
volume of public loans.[10]

As a result, there have hitherto been only four
periods in which the Bundesbank has conducted its
open market policy to a larger extent with longer-
term state debt instruments.   The first occasion
was in 1967, during the first severe recession the
Federal Republic had experienced;   at that time it
purchased about 1.3 Mrd. DM worth of fixed-interest
securities on the open market, with the aim of
pushing down interest rates.   After the upswing had
set in, in 1967, it nevertheless began to dispose of
these securities again, so that by the end of 1972
its holdings of domestic securities had declined to
a low level.   It was not until 1975, during the
second severe recession that had emerged after the
first oil-price-shock, that the Bundesbank purchased
7.5 Mrd. DM worth of public loans in the open market.
During 1976, however, this paper was again largely
disposed of in the market, mainly to offset the
foreign exchange inflows that took place in connection with the Bundesbank's obligation to intervene
in the foreign exchange market within the framework
of the European Exchange Rate Agreement.   Finally,
in 1978 and 1981, the Bundesbank once again made
large purchases of Federal loans, to the amount of
4.0 Mrd. DM and 3.0 Mrd. DM respectively.[11]

In general terms, the conclusion can therefore
be drawn that the open market policy of the Bundesbank has essentially one aim, to influence
conditions in the money market, and is conducted
with short-term money market securities.   Its mode
of operation and the supplementation of it by the
use of other flexible money market instruments has
already been discussed in the preceeding chapter.
Open market operations with longer-term public debt
have, in contrast, only taken place much less
frequently, and play a certain "outsider's role" in
the Bundesbank's utilisation of the monetary policy
instruments available to it.   Hence open market
policy does not, in the Federal Republic, constitute
an instrument with which to control the longer-run
supply of money in the sense of the fiscal components of the money supply.

2. Minimum Reserve Policy

The traditional instrument for the control of the
volume of central bank money already in existence is
minimum reserve policy;   it has in fact been employed for this purpose ever since the Bank deutscher
Länder was founded in 1948.   In the Federal
Republic, the minimum reserve obligations which must
be met by the credit institutions relate only to
their liabilities, and they vary greatly according
to the type of liability concerned.   Under section
16 of the Bundesbank Law, the Bundesbank can require
the credit institutions to hold with it non-interest-
bearing minimum reserves for current accounts, time
and savings deposits, with the exception of liabilities to other, likewise subject to the minimum
reserve rule, credit institutions.   For sight
liabilities, the minimum reserve ratio cannot exceed
30%, for time liabilities 20% and for savings
deposits 10%.   For liabilities to non-residents,
section 4 of AWG permits the imposition of a ratio
of up to 100%.[12]   Within these limits, the Bundesbank is free to adopt whatever reserve policy it
wishes, and can vary and differentiate the various
minimum reserve ratios in line with the policy
objectives it is currently pursuing.   Directions as
to the minimum reserves to be maintained are commun-
icated to the credit institutions in the form of the
socalled Order on Minimum Reserves (OMR) and their
currently prevailing levels are published in the
Bundesbank's Annual Report.
The Bundesbank also uses its power to differentiate between the reserves that must be held on
the various types of liabilities by posting

differing ratios for the level, origin and development of bank deposits. In addition, a few credit institutions of a special nature are exempted from the minimum reserve obligation. In imposing different ratios for the different types of liabilities, the Bundesbank is led by their respective degree of liquidity, so that the ratios are highest for sight liabilities. On the basis of the level and/or volume of the liabilities, three levels of reserves ("stages of progression") are distinguished between, with rising ratios coming into operation as the volume of the particular liability expands. Consequently, the average minimum reserve obligation rises continuously as the volume of deposits rises, once the first reserve level has been exceeded. The purpose of this provision is to promote the competitiveness of smaller credit institutions. A distinction is also drawn on the basis of the source of the deposits, to the extent that, because of developments in foreign transactions, higher minimum reserve ratios have occasionally been set for liabilities of the credit institutions to non-residents or particular ratios have been applied to the growth of such liabilities. Finally, at an earlier stage, the credit institutions had to meet higher minimum ratios if they were located in socalled banking centres, i.e. places in which the Bundesbank maintains a branch office.[13] This socalled "privilege for banks located in an area in which there is no Bundesbank office" (Nebenplatzprivileg) has been surrended since 1978, when the credit institutions were permitted to count their till cash towards their required minimum reserves. The following table presents an overview of the relevant minimum reserve ratios in operation since 1977.[14]

The credit institutions can meet their minimum reserve obligations - given the ratios in force at any time - in two different ways. Either the average is based upon all the closing balances of their liabilities subject to minimum reserve ratios between the 16th day of the month and the 15th day of the following month. Or only the closing balances of their liabilities on the 23rd and the last day of the preceding month, and on the 7th and 15th days of the current month, (the socalled "weekly bank return dates") are taken into account in calculating the average. To this "required minimum reserve" must correspond the daily average of the deposits maintained by the credit institutions with the Bundesbank during the current month ("actual reserve"). Since the credit instiutions need only

Table 5.1 : Minimum Reserve Ratios*

%'age of the liabilities subject to minimum reserve requirements

In force from	Demand Deposits Stages of Progression[1]			Liabilities to Domestic Residents Stages of Progression[1]			Savings Deposits Stages of Progression[1]		
	1 Up to 10 Mill. DM	2 10-100 Mill.DM	3 Over 100 Mill. DM	1 Up to 10 Mill. DM	2 10-100 Mill.DM	3 Over 100 Mill. DM	1 Up to 10 Mill. DM	2 10-100 Mill.DM	3 Over 100 Mill. DM
1977:									
1 March[2]	9.35	12.7	14.9	6.6	8.8	10.45	6.15	6.4	6.6
1 June[2]	8.9	12.05	14.15	6.3	8.4	9.95	5.85	6.05	6.3
1 Sept[2]	8	10.85	12.75	5.65	7.55	8.95	5.3	5.45	5.65
1978:									
1 Jan[2]	8	10.85	12.75	5.65	7.55	8.95	5.3	5.45	5.65
1 March	8.65	11.7	13.75	6.1	8.15	9.65	5.7	5.9	6.1
1 June	8.05	10.9	12.8	5.7	7.55	9	5.3	5.5	5.7
1 Nov	8.75	11.85	13.95	6.2	8.25	9.8	5.8	6	6.2
1979:									
1 Feb	9.2	12.45	14.65	6.5	8.65	10.3	6.05	6.3	6.5
1980:									
1 May	8.45	11.45	13.45	6	8	9.45	5.6	5.8	6
1 Sept	7.65	10.3	12.1	5.4	7.2	8.5	5	5.2	5.4
1981:									
1 Feb	7.1	9.6	11.25	5	6.7	7.95	4.65	4.85	5

Table 5.2   Liabilities to Foreign Residents

	Demand Deposits	Time Deposits	Savings Deposits	Growth in Liabilities		Savings Deposits	Provisions relating to growth in liabilities
				Demand Liabilities	Time		
1977:							
1 March	14.9	10.45	6.6				
1 June	14.15	9.95	6.3	no set ratios			
1 Sept	12.75	8.95	5.65				
1978:							
1 Jan	20	15	10	80			Additional Reserve
1 March	20	15	10	80			Ratios in excess of the
1 June	12.8	9	5.7				average level in the
1 Nov	13.95	9.8	6.2				period 16 September -
1979:							15 December 1977.
1 Feb	14.65	10.3	6.5	no set ratios			
1980:							
1 May	13.45	9.45	6				
1 Sept	12.1	8.5	5.4				
1981:							
1 Feb	11.25	7.95	5				

Notes: *Minimum reserve ratios before the rearrangement of the minimum reserve system in March 1977. cf. Monatsberichte der Deutschen Bundesbank, Table IV/1, pp 42*/43*. - 1. For the first 10 Mill. DM in liabilities subject to reserve requirements, the stage of progression 1 applies; for the next 90 Mill. DM, stage 2; and for sums in excess of 100 Mill DM, stage 3. - 2. Between 1 March 1977 and 28 February 1978, the following reductions applied for liabilities to domestic residents in places where there was no branch of the Bundesbank: for demand deposits 1%; for savings deposits, 0.5%.

adhere to the required minimum reserve on average,
they can temporarily use their deposits at the
Bundesbank for other purposes.   They will in fact
do so, and because their deposits with the Bundesbank bear no interest, the deposits they hold there
in excess of their minimum required reserves
("excess reserves") amount to only about 1% of the
latter.
      This very complex and differentiated instrument
operates in two main ways.   On the one hand, given
the minimum reserve ratios actually in force, it
creates a need on the part of the credit institutions
for central bank money, and in that way supports and/
or strengthens the efficiency of the other instruments - which are aimed at the creation of central
bank money.   On the other hand, changes in minimum
reserve ratios can be used to correct subsequently
the volume of central bank money already in existence.   When the supply of money by the Bundesbank
was based almost exclusively upon the foreign transactions component - as at the time of the Bretton
Woods system - minimum reserve policy was often
employed as the Bundesbank's "emergency brake," and
as the most important instrument for controlling the
circulation of central bank money in the Federal
Republic.   Variations in the ratios had, in addition,
an important signalling function, because the public
often regarded such variations as heralding changes
in the direction of monetary policy even when the
Bundesbank had not intended to do so.   In recent
years, with a flexible exchange rate against the
dollar and control of the money supply increasingly
aimed at stabilising its rate of growth, the frequency of changes in the ratios has considerably
declined.   In their place have been developed
methods of fine-tuning the money market which
operate upon the development of the supply of central
bank money in an essentially "more frictionless"
fashion.
      As a result, the signalling function of minimum
reserve policy has also experienced a decline.
Though the public has often demanded that the
Bundesbank should give up completely its use of this
instrument, it is doubtful whether it will actually
to so.   For the possibility of using it as an
"emergency brake" appears to very many practitioners
of monetary policy to be indispensable.

III The Operation of the Instruments of Monetary
Policy

1. The Concentration on Minimum Reserve Policy Until 1973

It has already been pointed out several times above
that at an earlier period it was the foreign component which was of decisive important in determining
the supply of money: this was especially so during
the 60's and early 70's. Whilever the Bretton
Woods system continued to be workable in general,
the inflow of foreign exchange reserves into the
Federal Republic stemmed almost exclusively from the
surpluses on its current account together with direct
investments from abroad. Domestically, the same
period was characterised by a relatively high rate of
growth of potential output at full employment and a
very high degree of price stability. As a result,
the task of the Bundesbank was essentially to maintain the agreed dollar parity of the DM and simultaneously to prevent the domestic banking system
from getting into an excessively liquid position.
It was able to do so without either massive intervention in the foreign exchange market or the
adoption of a series of restrictive measures within
the domestic sphere. It therefore restricted
itself - at least until the 1967 recession - largely
to using two of the instruments available to it,
discount rate policy and minimum reserve policy.
The latter served above all to put a subsequent check
upon the rise in free liquid reserves (excess
reserves, unused rediscount quotas and secondary
liquidity) arising from the foreign exchange inflows.
Since the maximum level of deposit rates was officially regulated until 1967, and bore a close relation
to the discount rate, variations in the discount rate
enabled a relatively direct influence to be exercised
on the behaviour of the non-bank sector.[16]

This "best of all possible worlds" in which the
Bundesbank operated, however, underwent a basic
change at the end of the 60's and the beginning of
the 70's, when the foreign sector became more subject
to disturbances and the Bretton Woods system went
into its gradual decline. In international
financial markets the expectation of an upvaluation
of the DM became widely held, with the result that
inflows of foreign funds into the Federal Republic
arose to an increasing extent not only from current
account surpluses and long-term capital imports, but
additionally to an ever larger extent from speculative capital movements. At the same time, the level

of state activity was considerably expanded. A
gradually rising rate of inflation ensued.

In these circumstances, the Bundesbank was not
merely forced to use its instruments in a basically
restrictive sense; rather, it found itself scarcely
able to exert the control necessary with its customary discount and reserve instruments. Discount
policy had become less effective because official
regulation of deposit rates had been eliminated in
1967, and, given the inflow of funds from abroad,
the credit institutions were really no longer
dependent upon getting discount loans from the
Bundesbank. Consequently, minimum reserve policy
took on in ever increasing degree the role of an
"emergency brake" applied by the Bundesbank: the
Bank used it to subsequently skim off the liquidity
flowing in from abroad under the system of fixed
exchange rates. Nor was the inflow checked by
either repeated upvaluation of the DM nor the widening of the band around parity within which the DM
was permitted to fluctuate. The Federal Government
therefore saw itself compelled to support the Bank
by imposing restrictions on capital imports under
sec. 23 of the Foreign Trade and Payments Law
(Aussenwirtschaftsgesetz, AWG). In February 1973,
all investments in German securities by foreigners,
and the larger part of the loans taken up abroad by
domestic borrowers, were subjected to the necessity
to acquire a permit to do so. In addition, from
March 1972 onwards the cash deposit requirement
(Bardepotpflicht) was introduced under the section
6a. which had been inserted into the AWG in 1971.

2. The Focus on the Foreign Exchange Rate and the Interest Rate Since 1973

It was not until the dollar rate of the DM was set
free to float in March 1973 that the Bundesbank
regained the freedom of maneouvre in the foreign
sector which permitted it to orientate its policy
instruments towards the domestic sector. Even then,
however, severe restrictions were placed upon it in
this respect by the agreements relating to the
European "currency snake", from which the "European
Monetary System" (EMS) emerged in 1979. At the
same time as it introduced the new concept of control
of the money supply - fully analysed in the following
chapter - the Bundesbank now increasingly attempted
to control the origin of central bank money by
measures directed at the interest rate, as against
the pressure it had previously experienced to skim
off - above all through variations in the minimum

reserve ratios - liquidity that had already come into existence. It also changed its methods to the extent that, to achieve a stabilisation of the rate of growth of the money supply, it intervened to a limited extent in the foreign exchange markets and the domestic money markets, and thus used this instrument more flexibly than it had done in the past. In the further course of the 70's, new means of influencing the money market - as already described - were developed for the purpose of controlling the money supply.

While the Bundesbank thus further refined its basic instruments of control, it was nevertheless soon confronted by new problems. These arose from the decline in private investment activity in the Federal Republic, which led in the course of the 70's to a rising trend of unemployment, as well as from disturbances in the international foreign exchange and capital markets, which especially at the end of the 70's originated in the monetary and fiscal policy being followed in the USA.

The deficiency of long-term, employment-creating investments had already made itself felt in the Federal Republic at the beginning of the 70's, though its consequences only later became completely clear. It was argued, firstly, that a whole series of changes had occurred which raised the need for a considerable increase in investment if full employment was to be maintained in the longer-run: the intensification of competitive pressure from foreign producers, changes in production methods arising from the adoption of microelectronic processes which replaced labour, and an annual inflow into the labour market which reflected previous peak years for births. Secondly, the phrase "insufficiency of investment" pointed to the fact that the rate of growth of investment in real terms had declined not merely relatively, i.e. with respect to the demands raised by structural change, but also absolutely.[17]

Fiscal policy reacted to the unemployment problem thereby arising with a debt-financed expansion of state expenditures. Public opinion called upon the Bundesbank to lend monetary policy support to this Keynesian demand - orientated fiscal policy, although a more careful analysis of the origins of the problem would have shown that the weaknesses in investment stemmed to a considerable extent from the supply side. As a result, the Bank refused to accede to these calls, all the more as it had since 1973 gone over to a strategy based on a money supply target (a detailed analysis of the money supply

target it adopted is presented in the following
chapter).   But what it could not prevent was that
to an increasing extent the public judged the success
or failure of its policy no longer in terms of the
behaviour of the rate of inflation but in terms of
the degree to which it succeeded in lowering
interest rates.   For a key role in the overcoming
of the weaknesses in investment was now attributed
to interest rates.

Powerfully contributing to the demands for low
interest rates was the fact that the Bundesbank
conducted its new money supply strategy above all by
employing the instruments available to it to influence interest rates.   It was through variations in
the discount and Lombard rates, as well as interventions in the foreign exchange and money markets,
that it sought to control the money supply.
Minimum reserve policy had previously signalled
changes in the direction of monetary policy;   this
role was now assumed in the public mind by discount
and Lombard policy.

Whilever the Bundesbank actually wanted to and
could utilise the degree of freedom in the external
sector conferred upon it by the introduction of
flexible exchange rates in 1973, the interest-rate
instruments for controlling the money supply worked
efficiently.   At first, the Bundesbank appears to
have possessed both the requisite desire and ability.
Certainly, the Federal Republic had already in 1972
adhered to the socalled "European Currency Snake",
the members of which had agreed to maintain fixed
parities between their respective currencies.   But
the obligation thereby arising to intervene in the
foreign exchange markets did not appear to seriously
limit the scope for the Bank to operate its interest-
rate policy.   The tendency for the DM to appreciate
against the dollar, which continued until 1978,
meant that the Federal Republic could uncouple
itself from trends in international interest rates
without substantially affecting the workability of
the "Currency Snake".   The relatively low level of
German interest rates in 1977, 1978 and still in
1979 nourished the belief that it was possible in
the long-run both to conduct domestically-orientated
interest-rate policy and simultaneously fulfill the
obligations arising from the European system of
fixed exchange rates.

But that this was merely an illusion became
evident at the end of the 70's.   What caused the
collapse of this monetary policy "dream", though
warnings had for some time been issuing from the

side of economic theory, was basically two events.
Firstly, the USA went over to a rigorous policy of
high interest rates: given the ever closer inter-
connections between the international financial
markets, this led to an increasing outflow of
capital from the DM (and from other European currencies) into the dollar, and hence to a depreciation
of the DM against the dollar. Secondly, within the
European Monetary System that had now been created,
the divergencies between the domestic monetary and
fiscal policies being pursued by its various member
countries widened. Hence the Bundesbank was ever
more frequently forced to support member countries'
currencies in the foreign exchange market, especially the French franc and the Italian lira. The
result was that expectations of a possible upvaluation of the DM against the dollar, which would have
been justified in itself in view of the greater
stability of the DM, were negatively influenced.
Consequently, the Federal Republic was no longer
able to escape the pressure exerted by the American
policy of high interest rates.

The obligations of the Bundesbank to continuously intervene in the foreign exchange market have
thus contributed to the fact that the Bank's
utilisation of its monetary policy instruments is
now once more decisively influenced by the development of the external situation, and to that extent
it is restricted in orientating its policy more
strongly towards the interest rate.

NOTES

1. Cf. Deutsche Bundesbank, Geldpolitische
Aufgaben und Instrumente Sonderdruck Nr. 7, pp 45ff
2. The quotas granted to each of the individual banks is not publicly announced by the Bundesbank.
3. Deutsche Bundesbank, op. cit., pp 48ff
4. Since November 1973, the Bundesbank has
with some intermissions also extended socalled
"Special Lombard Loans", bearing a "Special Lombard
Rate" which can be altered daily, while the facility
itself can be suspended at any time.
5. Cf. H.J. Jarchow, Theorie und Politik des
Geldes, Bd. II, Geldmarkt und geldpolitische
Instrumente, Göttingen 1973, pp 123ff
6. Deutsche Bundesbank, op. cit., p. 71
7. Hence in formal terms: $\dfrac{W_T - W_K}{W_K}$

where W_T = Terminkurs (forward rate), and W_K =

Kassakurs (spot rate)

8. Deutsche Bundesbank, op. cit., p. 83
9. On technique and institutional organisation, see the remarks on the money market in the preceding chapter.
10. At an earlier date, i.e. before the beginning of the income in public authorities' indebtedness in the mid 70's, the Bundesbank's abstinence from open market policy and operations in long-term securities was seen as primarily due to the fact that it did not have a sufficiently large portfolio of public debt instruments at its disposal. Since then, the volume of such debt instruments has considerably increased, and the Bank's continuing abstinence can no longer be explained in this way. Rather, it has become clear that the Bundesbank - despite frequent criticism from the public - regards open market operations in longer-term securities merely as a supplement to the employment of the other monetary policy instruments available to it.
11. Deutsche Bundesbank, op. cit., pp 68ff
12. Cf. our preceding remarks on the Cash Deposit Obligation (Bardepot).
13. The purpose was to afford some measure of relief to the places without a Bundesbank office: because of their distance from a branch of the Bank, they had had to hold relatively higher cash balances than offices in pla œs where such a branch did exist.
14. Extracted from Deutsche Bundesbank, op. cit., p. 57
15. See the table on p. 619 supra.
16. Cf. S. Oesterlin, "Zwischen autoritärer und marktwirtschaftlicher Zentralbankpolitik", in: W. Ehrlicher & D.B. Simmert, Geld- und Währungspolitik in der Bundesrepublik Deutschland, Beiheft 7 to Kredit und Kapital (1983), pp. 179ff
17. Cf. H.-H. Francke,"Konsistenzprobleme der Geld- und Finanzpolitik in den 70er Jarren", ibid., pp. 231ff

Chapter 6

MONETARY TARGETS IN THE FEDERAL REPUBLIC

I Monetary Policy under the Bretton Woods System

1. External vs. Domestic Stability
From the mid 1950's onwards, the Bank was faced
continuously with the need to attempt to "neutralize"
the domestic monetary consequences of large inflows
and outflows of funds from abroad.   These flows
resulted from continuing balance of payments surpluses and frequent speculative purchases of DM's
in the hope that it would be upvalued, and they
could on occasion be both very large in volume and
rapidly reversed within a relatively short period
of time as speculators took their profits on the
successful outcome of their speculation.   In the
earlier part of the period, this problem was not so
severe as it was later to become, because until the
late 50's the budgets of the public authorities were
in surplus, with the most famous example being
provided by the building-up of the socalled "Julius
Turm", i.e. the accumulation of a large volume of
funds by the Federal government in advance of the
expenditures that would be required to rebuild the
Federal Republic's armed forces.   Even during this
period, however, the money supply (M_1) rose by an
annual average of 11% between 1954 and 1958, or at a
rate exactly equal to the rate of foreign exchange
inflow during the same time.   While public budget
surpluses could do something to neutralize inflows
from abroad, therefore, the Bank was already exper-
iencing great difficulty in controlling the creation
of domestic liquidity.[1]
     The problem worsened from the beginning of the
60's onwards, and only two occasions in the subsequent period need be instanced to convey the order
of magnitude and reversibility of inflows from
abroad.   Thus, in November 1968 the Federal govern-

ment undertook an "ersatz" upvaluation by imposing
a special turnover tax of 4% on domestically produced goods and reducing by an equal amount the tax
on imported goods.   Far from discouraging speculation, however, this step was merely regarded as
announcing that a "real" upvaluation would soon be
effected, and between November 1968 and end-April/
beginning of May 1969, the Bank had to purchase
foreign exchange to the amount of DM 17 Mrd.   When
the DM was eventually upvalued by 9.3% in October
1969, a level of liquidity amounting to 21 Mrd. DM
was withdrawn from the West German banking system
within the next three months by foreign transactions.[2]
Again, in May 1971, the Bank had had to purchase
foreign exchange to an amount of 19 Mrd. DM from the
beginning of that year and in only three days of May
for 8 Mrd. DM.[3]
     The most obvious way of stemming these flows,
i.e. by variations in the exchange rate, was available to the Federal Republic only under the same
degree of inflexibility as it was available to other
adherents to the Bretton Woods system.   Of course,
not even under that system were exchange rates
absolutely invariable, and the DM was upvalued on
several occasions.   But such upvaluations were
generally small, and to carry them out often met
with significant political resistance at home, a
factor which still further intensified speculative
pressure on the DM.[4]
     The other main variable which might be mani-
pulated to stem such flows of foreign funds, interest
rates, was inextricably entangled both in the lack
of synchronisation between the monetary policies of
the leading industrial countries and in the conflict
between external and internal stability which the
Bank had so often to confront during this period.
On the former problem, the upvaluation of October
1969 was quickly followed by a widening interest
rate differential between the Federal Republic and
the USA, as monetary policy eased in the latter,
with a resultant large inflow of funds into West
Germany.   On the external/internal conflict, a rise
in domestic interest rates to check economic
activity in the Federal Republic stimulated foreign
inflows and opened up to the German banking system
the possibility of replenishing its loanable funds,
and at a cheaper rate, from abroad.   The converse
took place if domestic rates were cut to stimulate
activity at home.   Within the general framework of
stabilizing the value of money, therefore, the Bank
was often faced with a substantial degree of conflict

between external and internal stability.

The result was, firstly, that the ranking afforded by the Bank to its respective policy goals varied through time, as first one and then another of these goals appeared to be in most danger of disturbance. Thus, between 1958 and 1967, balance of payments equilibrium appears to have taken on dominant weight in the Bank's policies, while between 1968 and 1974 price stability was accorded that weight. Secondly, deprived as it was of one (or perhaps, taking into account the problems with the interest rate pointed to above, "one and a half") degree of freedom in its attempt to operate monetary policy, the Bank bore down all the more heavily on the other domestic monetary policy instruments it had at its disposal, a course of action which often involved it in substantial political conflict at home.[5] This, together with its views as to the appropriate intermediate target it should be attempting to influence, meant emphasis upon the use of instruments which influenced the liquidity of the banking system (minimum reserve ratios, gross re-discount quotas) as against those influencing interest rates.[6]

The range of instruments available to the Bank to conduct its policy have already been outlined in Chapter 5 above; our concern in the next section must be with the nature of the intermediate targets which the Bank sought to achieve with their assistance.

2. The Intermediate Targets of Monetary Policy

The Bank itself stated its aims thus:

> "Monetary policy in Germany is guided by the basic concept of controlling the banks' supply of credit, and the resultant increase in the money stock via bank liquidity and, in addition, of influencing non-banks' demand for credit by changing the interest rate level. The Bundesbank has a number of instruments for varying the banks' holdings of <u>free liquid reserves</u>..."[7]

The first step must therefore be to explain precisely what was meant by the phrase "free liquid reserves". We can then examine the consequences which the Bank expected to flow from influencing that target, and finally arrive at some conclusions as to the theoretical and practical appropriateness of that target.

A simple definition of free liquid reserves

(flr's) is that provided by the Bank itself: they
are "such highly liquid assets as a bank can convert
into central bank money at its own discretion", i.e.
their excess reserves, investments in foreign money
markets (with fixed exchange rates), holdings of
domestic money market paper, and unused rediscount
quotas.   The most obvious means of influencing
flr's possessed by the Bank were (a) to change the
minimum reserve ratios which had to be observed by
the banks, and thus the volume of their minimum
reserve deposits with it; and (b) to vary the conditions under which, and the cost at which, the
banks could utilize their rediscount quotas with it.
        So far as the former was concerned, the Bank
varied minimum reserve ratios on almost sixty occasions between 1948 and 1979.   There was as well an
interest-rate effect consequent upon doing so:
since the minimum reserve deposits yielded no
interest, a rise in them involved a larger proportion of the banks' assets being tied up in a non-
earning form.   With respect to rediscount quotas,
several opportunities were available to the Bank:
it could either impose qualitative conditions on the
banks' assets which were eligible for rediscount;
or it could fix absolute limits to their size; or
it could raise the cost of utilizing them.   (Conversely, of course, if it was seeking to bring about
an easing of credit conditions.)   It could as well
attempt to limit the banks' access to foreign funds
by direct action, through obliging the banks to
deposit with it a certain percentage of the funds
they had acquired abroad, although it did not
receive explicit legal authority to do so until
December 1971; or, finally, it could seek to limit
the inflow of foreign funds in general by various
methods, ranging from the imposition of higher
reserve requirements on foreign liabilities of the
banks to prohibitions on the acceptance of new
foreign bank deposits.[8]
        The traditional argument for controlling flr's
may be summed up in the phrase "credit control", for
what it aimed at was restricting the banking
system's ability to create credit by limiting to it
the supply of the liquidity which it needed to do so.
If it were successful in this aim; and if there
were a stable, regular link between the banks'
provision with liquidity, or rather changes in it,
and their activity in lending; then, controlling
the volume of flr's would enable the Bank to fulfill
its goal of influencing the supply of money and
hence the level of economic activity as a whole.

Whether in the period before 1971 the Bank
actually accepted the causal linkage in the precise
way it has been stated above is somewhat uncertain.
On the one hand, there are statements of the type
already quoted above, in which "monetary policy in
Germany" is said to be "guided by the basic concept
of controlling the banks' supply of credit"; on the
other hand, as Courakis points out, the importance
of this target is relativized by other statements by
the Bank, e.g. "The relationship between changes in
bank free liquidity... and the influencing of the
banks' capacity to lend.. is far from accurately
predictable".[9]   "Guided" would seem to have been
the operative word in defining the Bank's attitude:
it need not have believed that the causal linkage
was necessarily either highly stable nor highly
predictable, but it was the best target available.
So, faced with the enormous problem posed for its
control of domestic monetary expansion by the large
flows of funds from abroad, and locked into defend-
ing an exchange rate which was undervalued for most
of the period under discussion, the Bank perforce
operated on that source of monetary expansion which
it could most readily reach: the liquidity of the
banking system.   Certainly, its movement to the
new system of monetary targets after 1973 was
explicitly justified, at least in part, by evidence
that the relationship between flr's and banks'
supply of credit had "broken down".
Moreover, until that "breakdown" occurred, the
policy actually seemed to work in terms of the
Bank's overriding goal: the achievement of price
stability.   That it did so, however, might be
attributed not merely to the Bank's attempts to
control flr's but to the fact that those attempts
were being made within the framework provided by one
particular feature of the West German economy during
the period: a very high rate of domestic saving
because of restrictive fiscal policy and a relatively low rate of increase in real wages.   In effect,
then, the policy of operating on flr's involved
seeking to reduce the internal sources of increases
in the money supply in the face of continuing
external disequilibrium.[10]
Certainly, the Bundesbank would not have been
alone among central banks if it had framed its
operations in terms of checking the supply of credit
by seeking to control the banking system's liquidity.
Thus, a textbook of the 60's states that "major
emphasis in US monetary policy is on determination
of total money and credit supply by operating on the

cost and availability of bank reserves".[11]   In
Britain, on the other hand, the problem faced by the
Bank of England had bases somewhat different from
those affecting the Bundesbank: as the table in
chapter 2 shows, the "fiscal component" in the
growth of central bank money supply was very low in
the Federal Republic during this period, while the
Bank of England was faced with the problems posed
by a very large and continuously growing government
debt.   Yet, if the Bundesbank was inhibited in its
use of open market operations to influence interest
rates by the problems with foreign inflows pointed
out above, as well as by the narrowness of the West
German money market and the Bundesbank's lack of a
substantial enough portfolio of money market paper,
the Bank of England was likewise inhibited in such
operations by the obligations it felt to be imposed
upon it in its role as manager of the government's
debt.   Thus the Bank of England, just as the Bundesbank, sought throughout the period, firstly, to
control the banking system's liquidity by measures
aimed either at mopping it up or even more by
actually preventing the banking system from utilis-
ing that liquidity to make the loans and advances it
would otherwise have made.   Secondly, neither the
Special Deposits Scheme, introduced in July 1958 as
a means of immobilizing a portion of the banks'
liquidity; nor the ceiling on bank advances
employed on several occasions during the 'sixties
(e.g. in July 1966, the Bank of England announced
that "the ceiling on bank advances of 105% of the
level in March 1965 (would) remain at least until
March 1967"); nor, finally, the frequency of
requests for discrimination between differing types
of borrowers, had direct counterparts in the Bundesbank's activities, but the aim was the same in both
cases.[12]   And the parallel can be taken further:
when in 1971 the new system of Competition and
Credit Control was introduced in Britain, it was
partly supported with the argument that the previous
system of control had broken down.

II The Move to a Money Supply Target

The Bundesbank's movement to the adoption of a money
supply target occurred at a significant point in
monetary history, when the announcement of monetary
targets by central banks in several leading industrial countries took place at the same time as monetarist propositions were apparently gaining ascendancy

in both monetary theory and monetary practice.   It
was also a time when the collapse of the Bretton
Woods system of fixed exchange rates took place, and
the adoption of "floating" (albeit "dirty" floating)
in the foreign exchange market seemed to restore to
the Bundesbank that degree of freedom in its domestic
monetary policy whose absence had made its task so
difficult in the 60's.

In assessing the motivation for the Bundesbank's
change in operating policy, several problems require
discussion.   The first involves the reasons advanced
by the Bundesbank itself for its switch of emphasis
from flr's to the adoption of a monetary target, the
growth of the central bank money stock (Zentral-
bankgeld).   Second, the particular money supply
target chosen by the Bundesbank was not of the M1,
M2, M3 etc. type chosen by central banks in Britain
and the USA, and displayed some characteristics of
construction that raised questions among monetary
economists in the Federal Republic itself.   What
advantages, then, were claimed by the Bundesbank for
its own definition of central bank money, not merely
in relation to flr's but also to monetary aggregates
as defined and embodied in central banks' operating
practice in other countries?   Thirdly, once the
meaning and role of the central bank money target
has been clarified, it should be possible to assess
the extent to which the Bundesbank had accepted
monetarist propositions and based its behaviour upon
them.   Relatedly, there is the question of "success"
in achieving the desired rate of growth in central
bank money supply: did "success" mean that the
Bundesbank was actually able to bring about a rate
of growth in central bank money that fell within the
announced target range?

1. Free Liquid Reserves and Bank Lending Activity

Whilst it is tempting to attribute the Bundesbank's
move away from emphasis on flr's to a basic change
in its views as to the way in which monetary policy
worked, the fact is that the proximate cause for the
shift must be seen as the breakdown of the relationship between flr's and bank lending activity that
had apparently held during the 60's and on which the
Bundesbank's policy had been based.   In addition,
when the exchange rate was floated in Spring 1973,
the sources of domestic monetary expansion were now
apparently to a much greater extent within the
Bank's own control.   Certainly, both elements were
present in the argumentation with which the Bank
justified its shift in policy.

So far as the relationship between bank liquidity and credit expansion is concerned, that observed
during the 60's apparently ceased to hold at the
turn of the decade.[13]   What the Bundesbank saw as
happening from that time on, therefore, was that
banks' lending activity responded to an ever
declining degree to a reduction in their flr's;
especially, it could no longer be assumed that they
would be unwilling to see those reserves go below a
certain minimum level.   Rather, they began to
regard flr's not as a liquidity provision that they
desired to maintain at a certain minimum level, but
simply as an unused potential for expansion.   This
did not necessarily mean that e.g. a restriction of
flr's had no effect at all on the banks' ability
and willingness to expand their activities; but it
did mean that the choice of flr's as a strategic
target became increasingly open to the objection
that it was no longer clear what could be deducted
for the level of bank activity from changes in flr's.
What then needed to be cleared up was: what
was it that now primarily determined a bank's
decision to extend the credit it granted to borrowers?   The answer was that the key factor in its
decision was its estimate of its business liquidity,
which includes a very much wider spectrum of liquid
assets than those reckoned in flr's.   Thus, for
example, the banks included in their liquidity short-
term deposits in other credit institutions at home
and abroad; and these are assets which they can
create autonomously and, as well, whose rate of
increase is not limited by the obligation to hold
reserves against them.   Already in 1970-72 this
type of liquidity had increased at a much faster
rate than flr's.   Even more, however, the banks'
perceptions of the degree to which they are liquid
depended not merely upon the level of their liquid
assets relative to their obligations, but also upon
the extent to which they could acquire liquidity by
credit operations.   In this context, the growth of
the interbank money market at home and abroad was
pointed to in particular.[14]
In these circumstances, the Bundesbank concluded, the banks had begun to behave as though
liquidity problems scarcely existed: they relied
increasingly on the liquidity they themselves
created, their short-term interbank assets.   In
addition, they had learned that, even if the Bundesbank was operating a policy aimed at restriction,
inflows from abroad induced by interest rate
differentials or speculation could force it to create

central bank money.   Given this change in bank's
liquidity behaviour, the banks had to be shown that
there was still a unique limit to their expansion
which they could not overcome by their own actions,
i.e. the scarcity of central bank money.[15]
    Once the Bundesbank was no longer under the
obligation to support the exchange rate of the DM,
moreover, the source of liquidity which it had had
to struggle so hard to neutralize would no longer be
such a problem, and the possibility of conducting an
"autonomous" monetary policy was correspondingly
enhanced: the central bank could no longer be forced to create central bank money against its will,
especially at times when that action was indefensible
from the viewpoint of the stabilization of domestic
economic activity.

2. The Quantity of Central Bank Money

In 1974, the Bundesbank introduced the concept of
"central bank money", and at the end of that year
announced for the first time a target range for it
for the year 1975.   The quantity of central bank
money (CBM) was defined as: coins and notes in
circulation plus minimum reserves held by the credit
institutions on their domestic obligations at constant
reserve ratios, i.e. those in force in January 1974.
    The actual structure of CBM, and its relation-
ship to M1, M2 and M3 can be developed in the
following way.[16]   Thus, the first step is to draw
up a balance sheet of the overall banking system
inclusive of the Bundesbank:
    M1 and M2 are clearly derivable from the follow-
ing table, as is M3, and their components are de-
noted by the bracketed items.   The relationship
between CBM and M3 can then be shown thus (in terms
of the symbols used in that table):

1. Total currency in circulation (CC) =
    currency in possession of non-banks (CCN)
    and of banks (CCB)
2. M3 = M2 + SDIND
       = CNB + DPB + DRNB + TD4ND + SPIND, and
3. CBM = CNB + CCB + r_dTD4ND + r_s(SPIND +
    SD2ND)

The relationship between CBM and M3 can already
be seen as close, and, in fact, CBM can be regarded
as a weighted M3, where the weights correspond to
the minimum reserve deposits on various types of
bank liability in force in January 1974.   Thus, at
that date the average minimum reserve ratio for sight

Table 6.1: Assets and Liabilities of the Banking System As a Whole

Currency reserves
Loans by Bundesbank to non-banks
Securities etc.
Loans to non-banks

	Cash in circulation with non-banks (CNB)
M1	Deposits of private non-banks with Bundesbank (DPB)
	Deposits of resident non-banks with domestic banks (DRNB)
M2	Time deposits of domestic non-banks for periods of less than 4 years (TD4ND)
M3	Savings deposits of domestic non-banks subject to withdrawal notice (SPIND)
	Deposits of public authorities with Bundesbank
	Time Deposits of more than 4 years
	Savings Deposits with 1 year notice of withdrawal (2D2ND)
	Savings Deposits of more than 4 years
	Bond etc. issued by banks
	Other deposits

deposits was 16.6%, for time deposits 12.4%, and for
savings deposits 8.1%. This is shown in Table 6.2
    Three special features of this construct should
immediately be noted:[17] First, CBM is only <u>actual</u>
central bank money; items which constitute <u>potential</u>
central bank money are included in flr's. To recall
the definition given above, flr's are "such highly
liquid assets as a bank can convert into central
bank money at its own descretion". Hence, CBM
depicts monetary developments in the past to the
extent that these have been reflected in changes in
actual central bank money; moreover, it permits no
conclusions to be drawn as to future monetary
developments, since these depend upon the current
level of potential central bank money. Second, it
makes no allowance for foreign liabilities of the
banks, on the grounds that demand for German goods
and services by foreigners is not directly related
with the level of their deposits with banks in
Germany. Yet, as the Sachverständigenrat pointed
out,[18] deposits held by foreigners may well per-
colate into domestic deposits at times of monetary
restriction, and a substitution process of this kind
<u>would</u> affect the CBM on the Bundesbank's definition
<u>of</u> it. Thirdly, CBM does not include the excess
reserves of the banks because, in its words, they
"do not constitute the outcome of monetary expansion
but (rather) a part of the margin for expansion
still available for the banks". But as has been
pointed out, this proposition involves two further
propositions that are untenable: firstly, that the
holding of excess reserves must constitute an unprod-
uctive utilization of central bank money, and secondly, that the volume of central bank money already
employed in the currency circulation and as minimum
reserves on domestic liabilities cannot support any
further monetary expansion. Thus, in relation to
the second proposition, it is clear that, as
interest rates rise, the public responds by shifting
its demand for monetary assets from cash and current
accounts to other bank liabilities yielding a better
rate of interest, and these other liabilities are
subject to lower reserve ratios. As a result, even
if the quantity of central bank money remains unchanged, this shift opens up to the banks further
room for expansion.[19]
    Why, then, did the Bundesbank adopt such a
particular definition of the money supply as its
target? It advanced several reasons for doing so.[20]
First, it argued, which from among any particular
set of monetary aggregates should be fixed upon as

Table 6.2

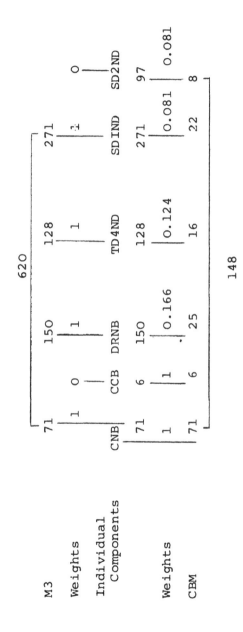

the targets would be a question of no importance if
the individual aggregates bore a stable relationship to each other, i.e. if they supplied similar
information as to monetary developments.   But experience showed that M1 and M2 at least showed substantial divergencies in their behaviour, because changes
in interest rates could bring about shifts of
deposits between them and at most the direction but
not the extent of such shifts could be predicted.
Certainly, British experience bore this out: in
1973, the annual growth rates of M1, M2 and M3
respectively were 9.9%, 12.2% and 25.3%;   but in the
following year, a very slight rise in M2 (to 12.6%)
was accompanied by a large fall in M3 (to 17.4%) and
a massive fall in M1 (to 3.5%).[21]   To the Bundesbank
this left only M3 and CBM as candidates.   M3, as a
broader definition, did not suffer from the problem
of interest-induced deposit shifts;   but because it
included so wide a range of financial assets in
addition to money, movements in it could not give
direct information as to the linkage between changes
in the quantity of money and changes in the demand
for goods and services.   Of course, the Bundesbank
conceded, it was not in practice possible to draw
any precise dividing line between money and other
financial assets, since what was involved was a
scale of decreasing "moneyness".   But CBM did at
least attempt to distinguish such assets by relation
to their degree of liquidity, and hence their ability
to serve as bases for the expansion of the money
supply, by weighting them in the manner described
above.   Finally, the Bundesbank advanced a statistical reason for its choice: CBM is derived from
average values in the course of the month and hence
is more quickly available than other aggregates.[22]
     The Bundesbank announced a target for a part-
icular monetary aggregate, CBM, which could be
closely related to M3.   In doing so, it therefore
adopted a practice similar to that of the Bank of
England, which, after beginning with a Domestic
Credit Expansion (DCE) target in 1968, moved to M3
during the 70's.   In the United States, on the
other hand, the Federal Reserve has set out targets
for all monetary quantity aggregates which can
deviate from one another, and has charged the System
Open Market Account Manager with achieving these
goals to the maximum extent possible.   The announcement of a single target clearly has several advantages: most obviously, if several goals are being
pursued with one and the same set of instruments,
the possibility of goal conflicts immediately arises.

And in the United States this problem has been
intensified by the addition of the duty to maintain
an appropriate Federal Funds Rate. Thus Burstein
has characterized the resultant Federal Reserve
operating policy as a "bastard system" of money-
supply control, "an illicit union of the schools of
the New York and St. Louis Federal Reserve Banks".
Federal Reserve credit is, under this system, being
supplied to or withdrawn from the money market
according to whether the federal funds rate is showing a tendency to move outside the targeted range;
at the same time, however, the consequences of this
activity for the supply of money are closely
watched.[23]
    Whether or not the advantages of announcing a
single target for expectation formation and behaviour by the economic agents have actually been
achieved in the Federal Republic and Britain is,
however, another matter. From the very beginning,
there have been substantial ambiguities in the
Bundesbank's CBM target, especially in its view as
to the possibility of controlling it and hence as to
the binding nature of any target once announced for
it. Thus, the Bundesbank specifically rejected any
claim that CBM was to be regarded as the "monetary
base" in the American sense: rather, it related
to the _employment_ of the central bank money made
available, and not to its _supply_. This is another
way in effect of putting the point already made
above: that CBM does not permit any conclusions to
be drawn as to future monetary developments but
reflects monetary developments in the past.
Secondly, in setting its CBM target, the Bundesbank
likewise specifically rejected what it took to be
the "purist" view that monetary policy could relin-
quish its anti-cyclical function, although it should
give more attention than hitherto to medium-term
aspects. Thirdly, the figure attached to the
target would have to be based upon a set of pre-
dictions as to the behaviour in the coming time
period of potential output, the degree of capacity
utilization, the velocity of circulation of money,
and an "allowable" degree of inflation, and the
opportunity for elements of discretion and perhaps
even guesswork to enter into this calculation is
obvious. Finally, in its attempts to achieve its
CBM target, the Bundesbank felt that it could not
leave to one side the fact that it _is_ a central bank
and has to carry a special responsibility for the
orderly functioning of the financial system. In
the short-run, it argued, the quantity of CBM

demanded by the banking system must be made available to them, and the central bank therefore must
create in some circumstances a quantity of money
greater than that which corresponds to their goal.24
Within two years of the adoption of CBM as the
operating target, the Bundesbank had relinquished
its view of CBM and flr's as alternatives: after a
period of time during which the Bank had followed
a policy of "flr's equal to zero", the CBM target
of 8% was in danger of being underrun, and the flr's
of the banking system had to be expanded.   When
all this is taken into account, it is difficult to
deny that Neubauer's characterisation of the Bundesbank's new policy contains a substantial element of
truth: the Bank operates today with the same
liquidity and interest instruments as it had already
used before 1972, and not in the slightest degree
does it seek to confer exogeneity upon its particular CBM aggregate.25   This conclusion is reinfor-
ced by the difficulties posed for the Bundesbank,
or rather by its response to them, in the late 70's
by the accession of the Federal Republic to the
European Monetary System, speculation on the DM and
international interest-rate differentials.   Of the
obligations assumed under the EMS, that which raised
most concern in the Federal Republic itself was the
duty now accepted by the Bundesbank to intervene in
the foreign exchange market to maintain the relationship between the DM and the other member currencies
within the agreed-upon range.   The Sachverständigenrat, for example, after discussing a long list
of fears that had been expressed about West Germany's
accesion, concluded that the EMS had little chance
of surviving unless monetary policy was harmonized
as between the member countries.26   For what West
Germany was now doing was to a certain extent
relinquishing the degree of freedom in its monetary
policy that it had apparently regained through the
transition to floating in 1973: the effect on
domestic liquidity resulting from foreign exchange
interventions would once again have to be neutra-
lized by the use of (e.g.) minimum reserve ratios.27
Furthermore, in the late 70's the problem of interest
rate differentials once again created a severe conflict of goals for the Bundesbank.   In 1980, for
example, an increase in the quantity of CBM would
have been desirable, both in view of its previous
tendency to decline and the recession of economic
activity in West Germany; but this would have
increased the interest rate differential between
the US and itself, with consequences familiar from

Table 6.3: Rates of Growth of Money Before and After the Adoption of Monetary Targets

	Average 1970 setting of first target Money Stock[a]	Annual average rate of growth % Average since setting of first target Money Stock[a]
UK	13	11
USA	6	6½
Canada	13	7
West Germany	9	9
Switzerland	7	10
Italy	18	23
France	16	13

a. For the USA, M1; for Italy, M2; for UK, £M3, but as this is not available for the period before July 1971, the growth of M3 is used as a proxy for the period 1970 July 1971.

Source: Brian Griffiths and Geoffrey E. Wood (eds.), Monetary Targets (London 1981), p. 29.

the pre-1973 period.[28]   Again, the problem with the
definition of CBM pointed to above, <u>i.e.</u> that it
neglected altogether foreigners' bank deposits with
West German banks, became of great actuality from
the late 70's onwards, as did the whole set of
issues raised by the rapid growth of what has been
termed "offshore" financing, especially through the
Euromarkets.   The appropriateness of the CBM target
became in these circumstances rather more questionable, and the Bundesbank itself from 1978 onwards
announced a range for its CBM target which in effect
inserted into consideration of the appropriate
growth in CBM the international interest-rate
differentials and the exchange value of the DM.[29]
    The nature of the Bundesbank's adherence to
monetary targets, and the characteristics of the
target it adopted, must therefore be viewed with
some caution.   But precisely the same could be said
for the Bank of England as well.   Thus, in his
statement setting out the new policy of Competition
and Credit Control in 1971, the Governor of the Bank
began by expressing disatisfaction with the system
of bank lending ceilings, coupled with official
declarations of priorities in lending, that had been
in operation almost continuously since 1965.   With
the aid of a very Tobinesque analysis, he pointed
to the "disintermediating" effects of such ceilings,
and laid down two lines for future policy: emphasis
on the "broader monetary aggregates... the money
supply under one or more of its many definitions.."
and a system under which "the allocation of credit
is primarily determined by its cost", <u>i.e.</u> the
interest rate, which meant a greater degree of
variability in interest rates than had previously
been thought appropriate.[30]   This is not the place
to embark upon a detailed description of British
monetary policy since that date, but four characteristics of it may be brought forward.   First, while
sterling M3 has been the target most referred to,
there has been "a restless search by the UK monetary
authorities for a definition of money supply which
is... meaningful in measuring the underlying stance
of monetary policy".[31]   Indeed, a constant theme in
pronouncements by the Governors has been that worth-
while information could be obtained by looking at
series of monetary aggregates other than M3, including monetary aggregates which embraced a much wider
range of liquidity.   There was no counterpart in
the Bundesbank's practice to this quest (Goodhart's
Law: once a particular aggregate has been chosen
for control purposes, it becomes unsuitable for the

purpose), but the constancy in definition of CBM was perhaps bought only at the cost of weakening its utility as an indicator.   Secondly, the Bank of England clearly does not accept the arguments for a monetary base method of operation, because it believes that the degree of variability in interest rates which would then occur would impair the stability of the overall financial system.[32] Indeed, it might be said to be sceptical of the extent to which monetary aggregates can be controlled: in Goodhart's words,

> "Most economic models take the money stock, or the high-powered money base, as given.   This is not the way it appears to the authorities. To them the control of the pace of monetary expansion often involves a difficult struggle ..."[33]

Thirdly, the way in which the Bank of England has actually conducted monetary policy since its adoption of monetary targets has been described by Friedman (naturally, from his own viewpoint of what would constitute correct practice) as an "egrerious example" of the way in which central bankers, while paying "lip-service to the control of monetary aggregates by announcing monetary targets.. have been continued to try to ride several horses at once by simultaneously trying to control monetary aggregates, interest rates and foreign exchange rates.." though the latter item of exchange rates has been officially disavowed since 1980.   For the British system has involved three components of policy: the interest rate, which is set exogenously;   the nominal money stock, the endogenous target variable;   and the monetary base, an endogenous variable adjusted by the Bank to provide the quantity of reserves demanded by the banking system.[34]   This is also, of course, the policy actually followed by the Federal Reserve in the USA.[35]   It is not surprising, then, that Friedman sees the Bank's practice as reflecting a confusion between money and credit.[36]

3. West German Experience with a Monetary Target
Although the Bundesbank adopted a monetary target at a time when monetarist policy concepts were beginning to exert a widening and even dominating influence in the field of monetary policy, its move was surely more a response to an apparent breakdown in what it regarded as its key instrumental variable (the flr's

Table 6.4

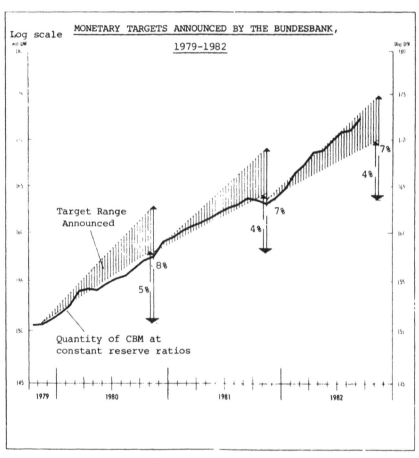

Source: Sachverständigenrat zur Begutachtung der
        gesamtwirtschaftlichen Entwicklung,
        Jahresgutachten 1982/83, Schaubild 25, p.83

of the banking system) and the opportunities for a
more active policy offered to it by the removal
from it of its obligation to support the parity of
the DM.   This presumption is strengthened by consideration of the particular target it chose and its
non-exogeneity, and its willingness to adjust that
target to enable it to pursue other goals when it
felt it necessary to do so. , In some years, its
target for CBM was exceeded by a large amount e.g.
in 1978, while between 1979 and 1982 it moved below
the corridor targeted by the Bundesbank for some of
the period, at the corridor's lower limit for
another part, and at its upper limit for a third
part, as is shown by the diagram 6.4.   Given what
has been said above about the ex post nature of the
CBM target, "success" becomes a difficult concept
about which to be precise in this context.
    What is also interesting is the implication of
the Table 6. : that the Federal Republic did little
if any better in constraining monetary growth after
its adoption of a target than it had done before
that adoption.
    In most respects, therefore, the Bundesbank
behaved in a way quite similar to that of other
central banks, even including the Federal Reserve
Bank where monetarist influence might be assumed to
have reached a peak.   Where it has differed from
other central banks is in the peculiar nature of
the target it chose and its autonomous conduct of a
monetary policy whose degree of restrictiveness
became at times an issue of political conflict, not
in any greater degree of adherence to monetarist
tenets as to the control of the money supply.

NOTES

    1. Helmut Schlesinger, "Geldpolitik in der
Phase des Wiederaufbaus (1950-1958)", in: Deutsche
Bundesbank (ed.), Währung und Wirtschaft in
Deutschland 1876-1975, Frankfurt a.M. 1976, p. 595
    2. Helmut Schlesinger, "Die Geldpolitik der
Deutschen Bundesbank", Kredit und Kapital, 11 (1978),
pp. 8-9
    3. Ibid., pp. 12-13
    4. See, for example, the controversy about the
revaluation of the DM in 1969: "Export als Ersatz-
Nationalismus", interview with Professor Giersch,
Der Spiegel, Nr. 21/1969, pp. 52-57

5. Hans-Peter Basler, <u>Wirtschaftspolitische</u>
<u>Zielpräferenzen und theoretische Orientierung in der</u>
<u>Geldpolitik der Bundesrepublik Deutschland.   Eine</u>
<u>Empirische Analyse des Verhaltens der Deutschen</u>
<u>Bundesbank</u>, Tübingen 1979.
6. <u>Ibid.</u>
7. Cited by Anthony S. Courakis, "Monetary
Thought and Stabilization Policy in the Federal
Republic of Germany", in: S.F. Frownen, A.S. Courakis,
M.H. Miller <u>et. al.</u>, <u>Monetary Policy and Economic</u>
<u>Activity in West Germany</u>, London 1977, p. 32
8. A comprehensive survey of the instruments
available to the Bundesbank to conduct its policy
is given by Dietrich Dickertmann and Axel
Siedenberg, <u>Instrumentarium der Geldpolitik</u>,
Düsseldorf 1979 (3rd. ed.).
9. Courakis, <u>loc. cit.</u>, p. 43
10. Hans-Hermann Francke, "Monetary Policy and
International Trade: Different National Strategies.
A Case Study: Japan-West Germany", unpublished
paper, 1982, p. 9
11. Eric Chalmers, <u>Monetary Policy in the</u>
<u>Sixties</u>, London 1968, p. 82
12. For a survey of British monetary policy
during this period, see J.H. Kareken, "Monetary
Policy", in: R.E. Caves and associates, <u>Britain's</u>
<u>Economic Prospects</u>, London 1968, ch. II
13. Courakis, <u>loc. cit.</u>, p. 36
14. Schlesinger, "Die Geldpolitik der Deutschen
Bundesbank", <u>loc. cit.</u>, pp. 16-18.   Schlesinger,
at the time Vice-President of the Bundesbank, may
safely be regarded as expressing the views of the
Bank itself on these matters, and also on the
issues taken up below with respect to the Bank's
justification of the particular monetary aggregate
it adopted as its target
15. <u>Ibid.</u>, "Neuere Erfahrungen der Geldpolitik
in der BRD"? in: J. Badura and O. Issing (eds.),
<u>Geldpolitik</u>, Stuttgart 1980, pp. 101-105.
16. The following draws heavily upon the
impressive work by Gerhard Förster, <u>Der Optimale</u>
<u>Geldmengenbegriff.   Eine theoretische und</u>
<u>empirische Analyse fur die Bundesrepublik Deutsch-</u>
<u>land</u>, Berlin 1981
17. Dieter Duwendag <u>et. al.</u>, <u>Geldtheorie und</u>
<u>Geldpolitik</u>, Koln 1977 (2nd ed.), pp. 55-56
18. Sachverständigenrat zur Begutachtung der
gesamtwirtschaftlichen Entwicklung, <u>Jahresgutachten</u>
<u>1974/75 "Vollbeschaftigung fur morgen"</u>, in: Badura
and Issing, <u>op. cit.</u>, p. 117

19. Manfred M.J. Neumann, "Konstrukte der Zentralbankgeldmenge", Kredit und Kapital, 8 Jrhg., 3 (1975), p. 332

20. Schlesinger, "Neuere Erfahrungen...", loc. cit., pp. 108ff

21. David Smith, "The Demand for Alternative Monies in the UK: 1924-77", National Westminster Bank Quarterly Review, Nov. 1978, p. 41

22. Schlesinger, "Neuere Erfahrungen...", loc. cit., pp. 112-113ff., 108

23. M.L. Burstein, New Directions in Economic Policy, London 1978, p. 54

24. Schlesinger, "Neuere Erfahrungen...", loc. cit., p. 74

25. Werner Neubauer, "Über die Unmöglichkeit einer monetarischen Geldpolitik", Kredit und Kapital, 10 Jhrg., 1 (1977), p. 74

26. Sachverständigenrat zur Begutachtung der gesamtwirtschaftlichen Entwickluung, Jahresgutachten 1978/79 "Wachstum und Währung", Stuttgart 1978, pars. 344-365

27. Leonhard Gleske (a member of the Board of Directors of the Bundesbank), "Die Devisenpolitik der Deutschen Bundesbank", Kredit und Kapital, 15 Jhrg., 2 (1982), pp. 262ff

28. Hans-Hermann Francke, "Die gegenwartige Zinsorientierung der Bundesbank-politik - Erganzung oder Gegensatz zur Geldmengensteuerung?", in: Hermann Göppl and Rudolf Henn (eds.), Geld, Banken und Versicherungen, Band 1,

29. Ibid., "Geldmengenpolitik bei aussenwirtschaftlicher Instabilität", in: Probleme der Währungspolitik, Schriften des Vereinsfur Sozialpolitik, NF, Bd. 120, 1981

30. Governor of the Bank of England, "Key Issues in Monetary and Credit Policy", Bank of England Quarterly Bulletin, July 1971, pp. 195, 196

31. Christopher Johnson, "M2 - the road to salvation?", Lloyds Bank Economic Bulletin, No. 44, August, 1981

32. For comment upon these and other problems that the Bank sees as involved in conducting monetary policy, see the first Mais lecture delivered by the Govenor of the Bank of England in February 1978: "Reflections on the Conduct of Monetary Policy", Bank of England Quarterly Bulletin, March 1978

33. Charles Goodhart, Money, Information and Uncertainty, London 1976, p. 152

34. D.C. Rowan, "Implementing Monetarism: Some Reflections on the UK Experience", Banca Nazionale del Lavoro Quarterly Review, No. 137 (June 1981), p. 123

35. See Henry C. Wallich, Monetary Policy and Practice. A View from the Federal Reserve Board, Lexington 1982, especially chs. 10-11

36. Milton Freedom, Memorandum, in: Third Report of the Treasury and Civil Service Committee of the House of Commons, Session 1980-1981: Monetary Policy, Vol. II: Memoranda of Evidence, p. 58

Chapter 7

THE FUTURE DEVELOPMENT OF THE SYSTEM

In this final chapter, some perspectives on the
future development of the West German banking and
financial system will be presented. As in other
countries, it will be subject to technological and
financial innovations, and faced with new tasks
resulting from changes in national and international
methods of making finance available. Monetary
policy, too, will thus be confronted with changes in
problems of interpretation and control, and the law
relating to banking will have to meet new regulatory
functions.
      In what follows, the emphasis will initially
lie on the technological and financial innovations
which are influencing the current development of
banking systems in most countries, and which in part
raise difficulties for the monetary policy which is
orientated towards traditional concepts of the
nature of a bank and of money. Next, we shall
point to the risks that the financial system is
clearly operating under, risks which present the
banks, but also banking legislation and supervision
of the banks, with new duties. Finally, some basic
considerations will be offered as to the particular
characteristics of the German banking and financial
system with respect to the question: to what extent
can this system be transferred to other countries?

I Tendencies in the Development of the Payments
System

1. Technological and Financial Innovation
While the conduct of business within the banks themselves and the transactions between them have now
for some time been subject to relatively continuous
rationalisation through the increasing utilisation

of computer technology, the relations between banks
and their customers are only just beginning to be
changed by the introduction of new electronic processes.   Yet there can be no doubt that in the
future it will be precisely this latter sphere of
bank business that will be subject to new developments.   What is noteworthy in the overall process
is that the technological innovations do not remain
confined purely to the technical conduct of payments
transactions;   rather, they simultaneously
constitute a presupposition for a stimulus to
financial innovations.   That is, they make possible
the emergence of new forms of monetary claims
between the financial institutions and their
customers.   Such financial innovations, above all,
to the extent that they give rise to means of payment, also bring considerable changes in the traditional concept of money: it is no longer a priori
clear just what money is, and what institutions are
to be described as banks.   Hence monetary policy is
faced with problems of changes in interpretation and
in control.
     The USA is currently the country in which
financial innovations are being most rapidly and
widely introduced.[1]   There are three basic reasons
why this is so: (1) the availability of new electronic technology has enabled a spatial decentralisation of payments transactions and an acceleration
in the speed with which they can be completed.   The
result has been the emergence of payments networks
which, on the one hand, electronically link the
"Point of Sale" (POS) directly with the financial
institution.   Consequently, in many cases (because
of the use of credit cards and similar media) cash
is neither employed nor transferred.   On the other
hand, to that the extent that cash is still employed,
its distribution to the banking public has been
mechanised (through automatic cash dispensers).
(2) The regulations relating to the financial system
have been outflanked by the market itself or by
changes made by the political authorities, or have
been completely eliminated ("deregulation"); the
former is true especially of Regulation "Q" which is
still in force, although introduced in 1933.   This
has led to the development of a large number of new
forms of deposit and new ways of calculating them so
as to evade interest-rate ceilings imposed by the
state.   The policy of high interest-rates in the
USA (at the end of the 70's and the beginning of the
80's) induced a greater degree of interest-
sensitivity among the possessors of monetary assets,

who thus sought to reap the benefit of that high
level of interest rates.

As a result of all these developments, so large
a number of new forms of payments and deposits has
come into existence that the phrase "bursting of the
dam" has already gained currency in this connection.
At the present time, emphasis should be given to the
i.a. following forms of financial innovations:

- "Automatic Transfer Service" (ATS)
  Through this method, the mutual savings banks
  offer individuals an offsetting service
  between savings and current accounts, paying
  interest at the rate for savings on deposits
  that would otherwise be held in non-interest-
  bearing current accounts.
- "Negotiable Orders of Withdrawl" (NOW's)
  "NOW's" are transferrable payments orders
  which are used in transactions just like the
  traditional cheque, but NOW-accounts bear
  interest.   Since they are issued by savings
  banks, they too can now offer their customers
  a type of offsetting account, though previously they were not able to do so.
- "Money Market Mutual Funds" (MMMF's) and
  "Money Market Certificates of Deposit"
  (MMC's)
  These involve deposits with investment companies and savings banks, which in fact yield
  a current money market interest rate and in
  part can be used for transactions purposes.
- "Repurchase Agreements" (RP's)
  These refer to the acquisition of cash or
  current accounts by the sale of securities
  with a simultaneous agreement to repurchase.
- "Sweep Accounts" (SA's)
  These are cash-management accounts with the
  broking houses: funds are transferred auto-
  matically on a daily basis between a transactions account and an investment account.

To this list of significant financial innovations could already be added still others, and a
further expansion of new types of payment methods
and deposits is foreseeable in the future for the
USA.   The same may be said for Britain, though the
pace of innovation there has been slower there than
in the USA.   But the banks have begun to develop
new interest-bearing current accounts (e.g. the
Cashflow accounts at Lloyds Bank) whose volume can
be expected to increase still further, and the

building societies are rapidly widening the range of
payments functions possessed by a deposit with them
(with the Leicester Permanent probably playing the
leading role in this respect).   To what extent have
such innovations been paralleled in the Federal
Republic?

Basically, a similar revolution cannot be
expected to occur in the Federal Republic, because
the presuppositions for it which are typical for the
USA but also in part for Britain are lacking in West
Germany.   Certainly, the technological factors
giving rise to such changes are operative in West
Germany as well, so that innovations which would not
have been made in their absence have already taken
place there or their initial stages can be observed.
That is true of the new technologies linking banks
and Points of Sale in association with a more efficient card system, especially the enlargement of the
functions discharged by the "Eurocheque card".
Similarly, automatic cash dispensers have already
been installed.   Above all, the future will bring
increasing possibilities of "home-banking" through
the linking of households by the cable system whose
beginnings can already be seen, i.e. the banks'
customers will be able, by using their domestic
televison sets (in connection with the socalled BTX-
System) to make payments and acquire information as to
new investment opportunities for their deposits.

But there are currently two further stimuli to
financial innovation in the USA: market or legisla-
tive deregulation and excessively restrictive monetary policy, and neither of these can be said to be
relevant for the Federal Republic.   Legally-imposed
ceilings on interest on deposits had already been
abolished there in the 60's.   Similarly, the Bundes-
esbank is able to control the target variable of
monetary policy, the quantity of central bank
money with a relatively high degree of elasticity
and stability, so that the very sudden changes in
interest rates which take place in the USA can be
avoided.   The result is that there is less demand
for forms of deposit like e.g. the Money Market
Accounts.   Most of all, however, the German system
of universal banking has always permitted all credit
institutions to compete with each other in all
markets.   Consequently, it has been able to offer
a relatively comprehensive range of services to its
customers without having to introduce the type of
financial innovations whose aim is essentially to
circumvent the regulation of interest rates and of
the system of banking specialised by function.   Put

briefly: in the Federal Republic, the bank customer can remain with his bank and utilise the type of means of payments which can be assimilated without difficulty to customary concepts of money, even if electronics brings considerable changes in future in the relations between the banks and their customers.

2. Consequences for Monetary Policy

The technological and financial innovations which have been described above and are to be observed above all for the USA raise some significant problems for monetary theory and policy, problems to which a solution appears at present unlikely. For the Federal Republic, however, they bear at best partial relevance. It might therefore seem justified to conclude that such problems for practical monetary policy are not of great significance for the Federal Republic and hence need not be discussed in greater detail. Yet such a conclusion would seem to be too simple and could even appear facile. For this reason, the problems raised for monetary policy that are of relevance to the USA will be briefly presented, before moving onto a discussion of the significance they might be expected to possess for the Federal Republic.

From the viewpoint of monetary theory, the changes to be observed in the USA throw up three essential problems:

- the problem that the customary concept of the money supply has become obsolete,
- the problem that there has been a decline in the demand for money as traditionally defined,
- the problem that the monetary transmissions process has become more interest-sensitive.

That the suitability of the traditional concept of the money supply has declined because of the financial innovations that have recently been made is due basically to one fact: the traditional - focussed upon the function of money - distinction between monetary claims whose essential function is that of means of payment and those which are means of financing, and thus function as means of storing money, is at best theoretically valid but is scarcely ever met with in statistical-empirical work. The functional linkage between a traditional trans-actions-orientated intermediate target for monetary policy (e.g. M_1 or M_2) and the ultimate targets of

Gross National Product and the price-level is, therefore, also empirically doubtful and cannot be utilised for practical monetary policy.

In Britain, too, the authorities have recently embarked upon the search for a new monetary aggregate which would behave more stably and exhibit a more reliable relationship to nominal GDP or inflation than those hitherto employed. Once again, the problem relates to the increasing difficulties posed by financial innovations for the traditional distinction between money as a store of wealth and as a transactions medium. Thus the new aggregate M2 is meant to measure "retail deposits" or "transactions balances", and attempts to catch in its coverage all other deposits (i.e. other than non-interest bearing bank current accounts) "on which cheques may be drawn or from which standing orders, direct debit mandates or other payments to third parties may be made".[2]

This unsuitability of the traditional concept of the money supply is closely linked with a decline in the stability of the demand for money in the usual sense. If at present in the USA e.g. more than 50% of M2 is made up of deposits which already bear the current market rate of interest although they can also be used for transactions purposes (cf. the following table 7.), it is as well no longer possible to detect any stable functional relationship between the M2 monetary aggregate and changes in the interest rate. Yet if a stable demand for money function is lacking, the arguments usually advanced for a steady control of the money supply in the sense of an intermediate variable are deprived of their basis.

Since the financial institions aggressively compete with each other for the deposits of non-banks, the mechanism for the transmission of monetary impulses has also become more interest-sensitive. The implication is that the risk of an erroneous steering of money aggregates has increased, and in the USA the question has already been raised as to whether it would not be sensible to return to an interest-rate intermediate target for monetary policy, or indeed to give up monetary intermediate targets altogether. Monetary policy would then be orientated directly towards ultimate targets such as the rate of growth of GNP. The same process can be observed at present in Britain, where discussion is said to be proceeding as to the desirability of setting targets for nominal national income as well as monetary targets.[3]

Future Developments

What is the significance for the Federal
Republic of such problems as these?   The proposition
has been advanced above that the technological and
financial innovations that can be expected in future
in West Germany will not raise such difficulties for
the concepts of the money supply usually employed
there.   But this does not imply that every one of
those concepts will continue to bear its present
functional relationship to the ultimate targets of
monetary policy.   In the Federal Republic, too,
new ways of making payments and holding deposits
will give rise to demarcation problems among the
monetary aggregates.   What constitutes an additional, significant difference from the difficulties
experienced in the USA and to some extent also in
Britain is that the problems thereby raised for
monetary policy are of a lesser order because the
intermediate monetary target employed by the Bundesbank, the quantity of central bank money, is defined
in a way that makes it essentially different from
the e.g. M1 and M2 aggregates used in other countries.
As has been shown in detail in the preceding
chapter, the "quantity of central bank money" (CBM)
is   closely related to M3, so that growth in it
largely coincides with growth in M3.   Like M3,
therefore, CBM is less sensitive to interest-
determined shifts between e.g. current accounts and
time deposits than is M1.   In fact, it is precisely
because M1 and M2 were always relatively sensitive
to interest-rate changes in the Federal Republic as
compared to the USA, and hence could not be controlled with a sufficient degree of precision, that the
aggregate CBM similar to M3 was chosen as the intermediate target.   With respect to its controll-
ability in the future, however, one problematic
aspect of CBM is perhaps the large proportion of it
composed by cash (50%, as compared with only 11% for
M3).   But if in the future - because of the consequences of new payments techniques - excessive
fluctuations take place in the cash component of CBM
as compared to its reserve component, this can be
taken into account by constructing a new weighting
for CBM.

If the need to do so were to arise, this would
naturally raise the question as to whether such an
intermediate target aggregate would still be sufficiently representative of the volume of monetary
assets available for financing transactions.   If
this were not the case, the control of this new
target aggregate to influence the level of demand
would become questionable.   It must once again be

pointed out in this context, though, that the Bundesbank's concept of controlling the money supply is relatively defensive in nature in comparison with that of other central banks, especially the "Fed". The Bundesbank aims more at the avoidance of incorrect monetary decisions than at directly controlling the ultimate target aggregates. In other words, the Bundesbank is always concerned solely to control the overall monetary framework than to exert a relatively precise influence in the short-run.[4]

Given this general approach, it is unlikely that the Bundesbank will in future give up its concept of controlling CBM in favour of control of the monetary base, the adoption of an interest-rate intermediate variable, or even more an exclusive orientation of its policy towards ultimate targets. The Bank has rejected the monetary base control currently being sought by many monetarists in the USA, because in the short-term it could confront the banking system with too great liquidity problems (which could make e.g. make them unable to fulfill their minimum reserve obligations). Such a method of control would therefore contradict the philosophy of monetary control "on a loose rein". There is no prospect that an interest-rate target will be explicitly substituted for that of the quantity of money, because a target of this type creates great risks precisely for a monetary policy which focusses upon stabilising the value of money and has to deal with disturbances of a real rather than a monetary nature (in the Federal Republic, above all from the sphere of the external economy). On the other hand, it does not seem likely that the Bank will cease to use intermediate targets, given the fact that its experiences with such targets has not been at all bad. In addition, any direct orientation towards ultimate targets would land the Bank in serious difficulties with political opinion: it would then have to make explicit decisions in favour of particular combinations of the ultimate variables growth, employment and stability of the price-level, and - even leaving the theoretical dubiousness of its doing so - this would intensify the pressure exerted by political interests upon monetary policy.

For all these reasons, it is safe to conclude that the Bundesbank will continue to adhere to its concept of control of the CBM for the foreseeable future. Yet it should not be forgotten that the width of the corridor in terms of which the intermediate targets are set leaves sufficient scope to

the Bank to orientate its activities over the longer-
run to other - unofficial - intermediate targets,
without lessening its credibility because of observed deviations from the official targets.   Targets
for exchange rates play the most significant role in
this respect, not merely because of the contractual
obligations imposed by the EMS but also from the
results of the empirical investigations of the
Bundesbank's reaction function.[5]   Above all at the
end of the 70's and the beginning of the 80's, the
Bank has on numerous occasions orientated its policy
more towards exchange rates than to developments in
the quantity of CBM.   Though from the viewpoint of
theory it is possible to advance numerous objections
to a policy of this type, the Bank can be expected
to conduct in future a - even if unofficial - policy
directed towards changes in exchange rates.

II New Risks in Banking

1. Risks in Domestic Financing

If the typical feature of banking business is seen
as the banks' mediation between the investment needs
of their depositors, more concerned with the security of those investments, and the supply of funds to
relatively uncertain investment opportunities, the
overall economic function of the banks then consists
in the bearing of financial risks.   And it is their
business to apply rational calculation to such
risks.[6]   To ask what will constitute the future
tasks of banking is therefore to ask: what will be
the new risks faced by the financial system and the
possibilities of the banks' assuming those risks in
the interests of their customers?
    The domestic lending activity of the credit
institutions in the Federal Republic has in recent
years been marked above all by growing risks of
insolvency among borrowers, risks arising in connection with the world-wide recession and the structural
adjustment problems faced by the German economy.
1981, with about 9000 insolvencies among firms, and
1982, with about 13000, represented postwar records
in this respect.   In addition to this quantitatively
alarming volume of bankruptcies and receiverships,
the attainment of also qualitatively previously
unknown dimensions was significant.   The "near-
collapse" of AEG, the second-largest German elect-
rical concern, was the largest case of insolvency
since the Federal Republic had come into existence.
The effect was to make clear to the public that even

large firms with "first-class names" were not exempt
from the risks of insolvency, and that they could
frequently drag down with them numerous smaller
firms dependent upon them. [7]
So far as the West German credit system is
concerned, the large number of insolvencies among
firms not merely implies that a large volume of
loans has had to be written off, because most of the
firms concerned had a high burden of indebtedness.
It also means that the banks - often under pressure
from public opinion and the politicians - have had
to advance considerable sums under reconstruction
schemes. This in turn directed attention to the
special features of the German financial system and
the risks thereby implied : the high proportion of
borrowed funds with which firms work, and the
dominance of the universal banking system. The
banks, in so far as they had direct participations
in the endangered firms, were subjected to two types
of public criticism at once. On the one hand, they
were said to have handled carelessly the deposits
entrusted to them; on the other hand, they were
accused of showing incompetence in the influence
they had exerted upon large firms through their
participations in them and the large sums they had
loaned to them.
In this way, those who had been sceptical about
the West German banking system could regard their
basic doubts as having been confirmed. Yet, it
must be pointed out that, despite the numerous fail-
ures among firms, the problems faced by the credit
system in mastering the need to write off large sums
of its loans have not been in any sense insuperable.
On the contrary, a whole series of examples can be
given in which banks have successfully worked
together in reconstructing failing enterprises.
They would probably not have been ready to undertake
such assistance if their involvement in the firms
concerned had not been so close. Looked at from
the viewpoint of the overall economy, the large
risks assumed by the banks through the high degree
of intermediation characteristic of the German
financial system simultaneously provided that chance
of bearing more easily the financial costs associated
with adjustment crises. Above all, as is shown by
experiences in other European countries, state
intervention on a larger scale has been avoided,
though it would otherwise certainly have been demanded by the public in view of the undesireable social
and employment problems created by the collapse of
firms. It can thus be argued that, even in a mixed

economy, a strong interpenetration of the banking
system and business firms makes it basically easier
to arrive at private economic solutions to adjustment crises.   The advantage of the latter type of
solution over state intervention is that in general -
but not always - they provide a more efficient
solution of the allocation problem.

Numerous occasions will doubtless arise in the
future in the Federal Republic on which the assistance of the banking system on a large scale will
become necessary for meeting the problems raised by
insolvencies and reconstruction of firms, for at
present no end is in sight to the national and
international employment and structural readjustment
difficulties that exist.   The current troubles of
the steel and shipbuilding industries and of coal-
mining can be mentioned as examples.   The tendency
to resort to state regulation of such industries -
especially with respect to the approaches adopted
within the framework of the EEC - is very marked in
other countries and their long-term success seems
doubtful.   The danger that exists for the future
is rather that the state will intervene to an
excessive extent.   Hence the flexibility of adjustment that the private economy can display represents
a structural advantage;   and such flexibility arises
in the Federal Republic from the close connections
that exist between the credit system and business
undertakings.

It must nevertheless be pointed out that this
structural advantage is not without costs of its
own.   If, as in the Federal Republic, banks to a
considerable extent bear the risks of the productive
and investment activity of business firms because
of the high degree of intermediation in the
financial system, the costs of assuming these risks
must be covered by the banking system's attaining a
corresponding level of earnings.   In other words,
to an inter-sectoral transformation of risks - from
the business to the banking sector - there must
correspond an inter-sectoral earnings transformation,
if the basic financial strength of the credit system
itself is not to be endangered.[8]

The rise in the differential between the interest rates charged and paid by the banks that is
necessary for this purpose can occur by means of
either a rise in the interest paid by firms on their
borrowing or a reduction in the interest paid by
banks on their deposits.   Which will take place is
determined by competition in the market.   In the
past, at any rate until the end of the 70's, deposit

rates especially were at a level in the Federal
Republic which was very low, both absolutely and by
international comparison. The permanent tendency
of the DM to appreciate was one of the factors which
made this possible. But it seems doubtful that this
state of affairs will continue to prevail in the
future. The greater degree of mobility in international finance markets and the growth in state
indebtedness in recent years have made the deposits
of the broad banking public as well much more
sensitive to interest rates. Yet if the banks are
no longer able to shift their risk costs onto their
depositors via lower deposit rates, and instead the
rates on loans will have to rise, the current adjustment problems of the West German economy will be
considerably intensified in light of the high level
of indebtedness of many firms. This constitutes
perhaps one of the greatest risks currently faced
by the financial system in the Federal Republic.

2. Risks in International Lending

We have already mentioned on several occasions the
risks presently confronting international lending
activity because of the over-indebtedness of numerous developing countries and centrally-planned
economies, so they need only briefly be discussed
here. While the banks of a number of other
countries are affected in a similar way by the
problems that thereby arise, there are some particular features of the position of the West German
banks which should be emphasised. First, the
German credit institutions have made loans to the
East European centrally-planned economies to a much
larger amount than have banks in other countries.
This has been due on the one hand to the traditionally close trading relations - determined by geo-
graphical position - between the German economy and
Eastern Europe. On the other hand, political
motives have been important, for the Federal
government promotes relations of this kind within
the framework of its policy of detente vis-a-vis the
Communist countries. But since the centrally-
planned economies are afflicted by a chronic shortage of foreign exchange, trade with them is in
general made possible only by additional credit
financing. To that extent the Federal government
has an interest in West German banks' involvements
in Eastern Europe, and large credits have been made
available in the past by West German banking
consortia very frequently under state mediation and
with state intercession. Loans to Poland and the

GDR can be instanced in this connection.

The risks run by the banks in lending to East European countries differ basically in two respects from those involved in loans to developing countries. First, the security of such loans depends decisively upon general political developments. Political conflicts within the centrally-planned economies, as e.g. in the case of Poland, can very quickly endanger their ability to repay the loans. In addition, political tensions between East and West raise the risk that the loans either cannot or may not be repaid. Second, it cannot be expected that organisations such as the IMF will mount international support schemes if such countries become unable to pay. The socalled "umbrella theory" argued that, on the basis of socialist solidarity, the Soviet Union would always and unrestrictedly assist its Eastern Bloc partners if they get into financial difficulties; but it has not shown itself to be operative in the past.[9]

The future economic and political development of East-West relations consequently assumes considerable significance for the West German banking system as well. At the moment, a voluntary and comprehensive disengagement by West German banks from their credit business with the East European economies cannot be expected. If they were compelled to do so by political factors, considerable adjustment problems could arise for them and they would probably call upon state assistance.

The second particular aspect of the West German banks' international lending activity concerns their demands on highly-indebted developing countries. This does not refer to the problem of the threatening inability to pay of individual countries, for lenders in other countries are in a similar position. The German banking system's additional difficulties arise from the fact that German banks have lent to developing countries basically through their foreign subsidiaries, over which the Federal banking supervisory system has little control. This has meant, however, that the risk position of the West German mother bank as well has become increasingly difficult to ascertain, and the possibility of acting so as to diminish it is small in the absence of any legal norms which could be called upon to do so. Changes in this respect are certainly likely in the future, and we shall return to them below.

3. Risks Arising from Changes in Monetary Policy

In addition to the risks in national and international lending, there are those which arise for
the banks above all through unforeseeable changes in
monetary and fiscal policy. So far as concerns the
employment of monetary policy weapons primarily for
domestic economic reasons - if that use can be
isolated in an open economy such as the Federal
Republic - a considerable advance has been made in
recent years in the direction of greater continuity
and hence predictability. The new instruments of
the Bundesbank relevant in this context, especially
with respect to its interventions in the money
market, have been described in detail in preceding
chapters. Unfortunately, the external economic
component of monetary policy has not displayed the
same positive development. The experience of
recent years shows, rather, that in this field new
risks have emerged, and the banks have still an
arduous learning process to undergo before they are
able to handle them.

First to be emphasised in this context is
exchange rate risks. They result not merely from
the fact that since 1973 the DM has floated against
other important currencies such as the dollar and
the pound sterling. Certainly, the behaviour of
completely flexible exchange rates in the short
period can scarcely be predicted within the theoretical framework currently available; but the
movements of exchange-rate parities in the medium
and longer-term would be able to be foreseen if
sufficient information could be acquired as to the
behaviour of monetary policy. But it is precisely
this which is lacking. For one thing, the DM is
relatively firmly linked to the other currencies in
the EMS, so that its exchange rate against e.g. the
dollar fluctuates not merely under the influence of
market forces but also in dependence upon the intervention obligations agreed under the EMS. In
addition, as has already been pointed out on several
occasions, the Bundesbank has always pursued - if,
of course, this aim has not been officially
announced - short-term exchange rate targets in
addition to the CBM target.

The exchange risks of the banks are intensified
by this type of Bundesbank intervention in the
foreign exchange market because it draws out the
process in which predicted market trends are actually
realised. Moreover, it frequently takes place in
such a discontinuous fashion that its influence upon
exchange rate parities becomes unpredictable. For

the banks, the important consequences which thereby
arise are not so much that the value of their
deposits abroad changes in an unpredictable way, but
above all that they are subjected to an increased
risk of interest rate charges by the greater
exchange rate risks they must confront.[10]   The
reason is that, given freedom of international
capital flows, differences in interest rates between
the various countries are determined predominantly
by expectations of changes in exchange rates.
Hence a rise in the risk of exchange rate changes
must also intensify the risk of interest rate
changes.
      The latter factor is of especial significance
for the West German banking system because the
universal bank which dominates it is heavily
involved in maturity transformation between deposits
and loans.   But a rising risk of interest-rate
changes also means greater risks in maturity transformation.   For then the banks have increasingly to
take into account the possibility that they may have
in the meantime to refinance at higher interest
rates the loans they have made over a longer term,
and such rates may exceed the level they predicted
and thus involve losses.   To the extent that these
dangers have been recognised, they have been reflected in a shortening of the period for which loans
are granted or the introduction of such innovations
as "roll-over credits".   The banks have sought in
any case to transfer to their borrowers the
increased risk of interest-rate changes, with detrimental effects upon their investment activity.
      The instability in the international foreign
exchange and financial markets has thus had considerably damaging effects upon the West German banking and financial system.   If they continue to be
operative in the future, the danger exists that the
West German universal banking system will lose a
significant element in its effectiveness, involved
as that system is in maturity transformation.   The
solution to this problem is to be found, however,
not merely in a greater degree of calculability in
the Bundesbank's mode of behaviour in the foreign
exchange markets, but also and above all in greater
consistency in the policy of the US central bank.

III Problems of Bank Supervision and Legislation

1. The Problem of Capital Resources
"The ability of the banks to bear risks is ultimately

determined by the capital resources they possess",[11] as the Study Group on Basic Issues in the Credit System remarked in its report of 1979. The Federal Economics Minister, Otto Graf Lambsdorff, was even more pointed in his statement to the German Savings Banks Annual Conference in 1976: "Whoever does not possess adequate funds should not carry on banking business!". His speech must be seen within the context of the revision of banking legislation under discussion at that time in the Federal Republic, which was concerned with among other things the question of new provisions as to the capital resources to be required of the credit institutions. Behind these discussions lay a two-fold problem: firstly, the basic belief of critics of West German legislation that the German credit institutes' capital resources were in general too low and did not reach the international standard of about 5% of their balance sheet totals (even among the large banks). Secondly, from within the credit system itself, the criticism was voiced that publicly-owned credit institutions in particular but the cooperative sector as well were operating with too low a level of capital resources, a dangerous procedure in view of their expanding activity in the fields of industrial credit and foreign business.

The West German credit institutions' capital resources do in fact appear to be small – and not merely by international standards – if the new risks in banking referred to above are taken into account, and especially if attention is focussed upon the participation risks to which the universal banking system gives rise. Thus, every participation by one credit institution in another brings with it additional possibilities of extending credit without new capital funds having to be provided for the purpose. Complex pyramids of credit can originate in this way and have already done so in the sphere of foreign business. From the viewpoint of the overall economy this seems a hazardous procedure, for the possession of a low level of capital resources by the banks restricts their ability to bear losses from their own resources. Bank collapses at times of crises therefore become a possibility, which can then give rise to amplified repercussions within the overall financial system. An additional point is that too low a level of capital resources on the part of banks active in the international sphere reduces their "standing" in dealings with foreign banks, with detrimental effects upon the West German economy as a whole, involved as that economy is in international trading competition.

The West German banking system's problems with capital funds is due essentially to two factors: first, the universal banking system itself seems to give rise to a tendency towards a low owned-capital/ volume of business ratio. The reason is to be found in its two particular characteristics: the drive for expansion, and intensive competition. This encourages the propensity to neglect the building-up of capital funds, at least during economic "fair weather periods" enduring for some time. The second factor is the basic nature of banking policy and legislation in West Germany. Since the beginning of the 1930's, the principle under which German banking policy has operated has been "the preservation of the efficiency of the banking system by safeguarding the existence of the credit institutions through an extensive system of legal norms".[12] As a result, the consciousness of risk and "feeling of liquidity" among the German credit institutions has developed in a completely rational accommodation to existing banking legislation. Hence "the volume of capital resources has ceased to possess significance as a basis for the determination of the extent of banking business" and is scarcely any longer regarded as a reserve against risk, the possibilities of loss of which should induce caution in the taking-on of new risks.[13]

But it is difficult to depart from traditions, especially when they have given rise to structures which have developed over a long period and changes in them must involve high costs and losses of influence by particular interests. The Study Commission entrusted with the preparation of amendments to the banking legislation has thus also rejected the basic criticism levelled against the low capital resources of the West German banks. That legislation has likewise remained anchored to its maxim of safeguarding the existence of the credit institutions by means of differentiated structural norms applied to their balance sheets, instead of introducing a basic reorganisation of the mechanism for balancing net worth and risks. The only change that was made related to an aspect of the system which was regarded as especially important from the viewpoint of competition: the advantages allegedly possessed by the savings banks and the cooperatives were lessened by to some extent assimilating the provisions under which they operated to those of the

other credit institutions.[14]   The West German banking system will therefore continue to have in future
a low level - by international standards - of
capital resources.   To dismiss as irrelevant the
problems that could thereby possibly emerge would be
irresponsible, and it can only be hoped that future
tasks and risks will nevertheless be able to be
mastered without more serious difficulties arising.

2. Problems of Information as to Foreign Involvements.
Closely related to the problem of capital funds are
the difficulties faced by the banking supervisory
authorities which stem from the internationalisation
of banking business.   For a significant part of the
capital funds problem consists in the fact that the
volume of liabilities against which the West German
banks' capital resources are liable is multiplied if
these banks are also operating through foreign
subsidiaries.   If their foreign involvements are
to be brought within the framework of bank supervision and legislation, the creation of an obligation on the part of the banks to provide this
information is essential, though hitherto it has not
been introduced.

At present, all that exists is a type of
"gentlemen's agreement" between the banks and the
West German controlling authorities: the banks have
voluntarily accepted the obligation to make available data relating to their foreign subsidiaries.
The Federal Banking Supervisory Authority is in this
way to gain an overview of the total lending commit-
ments entered into by the German parent banks and
their foreign subsidiaries.   But naturally this is
an unsatisfactory situation, for it seems reasonable
to fear that a bank will refuse to make information
available precisely when such information would land
it in difficulties with the Supervisory Agency.   It
therefore cannot cause surprise that the State
Secretary in the Federal Ministry of Finance, Hans
Tietmayer, recently declared: "The longer the
gentlemen's agreement has existed, the clearer it
has become to me that a legal settlement of the
issue is necessary, so that the obligation of the
banks to provide information is put upon a proper
legal basis".   Indeed, it now appears to be the
intention of the Federal government to replace this
voluntary agreement by a compulsory obligation of
the banks to supply the information involved.[15]

The West German banks should welcome a legally
laid-down reporting duty of this kind, for at least
two reasons.   On the one hand, all West German banks

would be forced into a single framework of operations for their foreign business as well, which would
put the competition between them onto an objective
basis.   This would be of significance not merely
for that foreign business itself but for competition
between them on the domestic market as well.   For a
bank can frequently transact domestic business only
if it can offer its domestic clients additional
service for their foreign transactions.   On the
other hand, and certainly more importantly, the
confidence of foreign banks and businesses in
Federal Republic banks would be consolidated if their
external relations as well were subject to the regu-
lative framework of the banking supervisory authorities.   The negative experiences with the collapse
of the Herstatt Bank still seem to have adverse
effects upon the image of West German banks that is
held abroad.
        Yet the question is still completely open as to
the use that can and should be made by the Federal
Banking Supervisory Agency of the information it
would acquire from an extension of the banks' duty
to report on their foreign involvements.   A first
step might be for the authorities to exercise merely
an advisory and cautioning influence upon the banks
concerned.   They would therefore notify the banks
of any risky developments they believed they had
observed, and ask the banks for information as to
the precautions they themselves were taking.   In
this case, the authorities would not apply supervisory regulations or restrictions upon the banks
involved, and such a procedure would be totally in
line with the pragmatic style of bank supervision
in the Federal Republic.[16]   It seems doubtful, .
however, whether any wider-reaching steps will be
possible in the foreseeable future, since the magnitude of the risks in foreign lending is so great
and there has hitherto been a lack of analysis and
of agreement - internationally as well - as to how
these risks can be limited.[17]

        Can the West German System be Transferred to
Other Countries?

The discussion of foreign economic systems is frequently a source of interest because it is linked -
explicitly or implicitly - with the question: could
it be useful for one's own economy as well to take
over from other economies modes of behaviour and
regulations that have proved successful there?;   or

would it not be possible to come up with an efficient solution to one's own difficulties and problems
by "importing" a system that has been efficient
elsewhere? At a time when wide-reaching changes
are taking place precisely in the banking and financial systems of numerous countries, changes which
create significant challenges for monetary regulat-
ive and process policy, a further question suggests
itself: to what extent can the West German banking
and financial system serve as a model for other
countries? We shall conclude this book with a
brief attempt to answer this question.

The authors of this book believe that there are
very narrow limits set to the international trans-
ferability of economic systems, and that any attempts to do so should be viewed with the utmost
scepticism. The reason is, simply, that people
cannot be exported, a proposition that may sound
trivial but is in fact of basic significance. The
ability of economic systems to function rests upon
the fact that the people active within them make
their decisions on the basis of information which
they evaluate in terms of their own specific historical experiences, and transform those decisions
into particular modes of behaviour without having on
every occasion to carry through a comprehensive,
objective analysis. On the contrary, in general it
is true to say that rational economic behaviour is
possible even in the absence of a very wide range of
information being available, if this is measured in
terms of the immense number of economic processes
that are taking place simultaneously in an economic
system. But this reduction in the need for current
information can occur only because historical experience enables people to handle information rationally
and calls forth in them modes of behaviour which have
developed historically. As beings of an historical
nature, people in one economy differ from those in
other economies. Hence the introduction of new
data into the economic framework not merely evokes
adjustment processes that are expensive in terms of
time. Even more, because they impinge upon what
have been characteristic modes of behaviour, they
give rise to reactions which frequently differ from
those that have been observed in other countries in
response to similar changes. That does not mean
that economic man is not a world citizen who is
capable of learning; it does mean that as a rule he
has at the same time a particular nationality which
bears the stamp of history and is not exchangeable
at will for another.

162

Future Developments

From this aspect, it seems doubtful that economic system and structure can be efficiently transferred across national boundaries. The comparison of different national systems may give some general indications of the developments and possible solutions that can be expected, but account must always be taken of the specific, historically-developed characteristics of any particular country. If the West German banking and financial system is considered from this angle, two general features of it appear to be relevant to other countries. Firstly, in comparison with the more strictly regulated systems of banking specialised by function in England and especially in the USA, it is an advantage if - as in the West German universal banking system - intensive competition is possible in the credit system. This is because, in the long-run, a policy of regulation which restricts competition and thus the earnings prospects of the banks cannot be maintained without efficiency losses in the form of efforts to evade the regulations. The attempts at subsequent deregulation may then lead to sudden upheavals which confront monetary policy with scarcely soluble tasks. Secondly, West German experience also shows that a universal banking system has a tendency to wide-ranging expansion, implying the danger of an undesirable amassing of power by the banks. The competition between public, private and cooperative credit institutions that has developed historically in the Federal Republic certainly works against any one-sided accumulation of power. But this "three-pillar-system" appears neither to be able to be transferred abroad without any further ado, nor is it suitable by itself to secure public control and information. For this, the adjustment of the system of bank supervision to new developments is a task that must ever again be undertaken.

NOTES

1. A survey of the changes in the financial and banking system can be found in the journal Contemporary Policy Issues, No. 2, January 1983, containing articles by P.M. Laub and Ch. F. Hoffmann, K.J. Thygerson, and J.L. Pierce.
2. For a brief but informative discussion of the thinking underlying the search for a new target monetary aggregate, see Christopher Johnson, "M2 - The road to salvation?", Lloyds Bank Economic Bulletin, No. 44, August 1982.

3. Frances Williams, "Time to bend the text-book rules of monetarism", The Times, 20 October 1983

4. On this point see H. Bockelmann, "Orient-ierungspunkte der Geldpolitik", forthcoming in Kredit und Kapital

5. Cf. e.g. M.J.M. Neumann, "Intervention in the Mark/Dollar Market: The Authorities' Reaction Function", Paper prepared for the Konstanz Seminar on Monetary Theory and Monetary Policy, 1983

6. See W.D. Becker, "Changing Dimensions of Banking Tasks", in: Landesbank-Girozentrale Rheinland-Pfalz (ed.), Banken, Festschrift zum 25-jährigen Bestehen, Frankfurt a. M. 1983, pp. 169 ff

7. L. Huber, "Neue Risiken im Bankgeschäft", p. 97 in: Landesbank-Girozentrale Rheinland-Pfalz, op. cit., pp. 95ff

8. In this connection, see H.H. Francke, "Intersektorale Risikotransformation und private Investitionstätigkeit", Schriften des Verbandes öffentlicher Banken, Heft 1 (1977), pp. 42ff

9. Huber, loc. cit., p. 107

10. Becker, loc. cit., pp. 169ff

11. Ibid.

12. See L. Mühlhaupt, "Von der Bankenkrise 1931 zur Bankenaufsicht 1981", Zeitschrift fur bankw. Forschung 34 Jg. (1982), p. 441

13. Becker, loc. cit., pp. 169ff

14. The current prospect is that the KWG will be amended in this area in the course of 1983. It seems likely that the concession previously enjoyed by both the public credit institutions (especially the savings banks) and the credit cooperatives, under which the capital plus reserves and retained profit has been enlarged by the amount of members' uncalled liabilities, will be abolished. The purpose is to subject all credit institutions to the same require-ments in this respect.

15. See Die Zeit, No. 28 vom 8 Juli 1983, p. 19, the article by Rudolf Hertl, "Stoltenberg vor heissem Herbst"; Rudolf Hertl, "Eigentor der Banken", Die Zeit, No. 42, 14 Oktober 1983, p. 29

16. Cf. J.L. Bähre, "Die Herausforderung der Bankenaufsicht", in: Landesbank-Girozentrale Rheinland-Pfalz (ed.), op. cit., pp. 13ff

17. Symptomatic in this connection appears to be the statement of the socalled Cooke Committee, set up at the Bank of International Settlements to develop criteria by relation to which country risks may be dealt with. It writes: "A bank should spread its risks among various countries; but the

Future Developments

Committee is aware that there may be professional
knowledge about particular countries and groups of
countries which makes lending to only a few
countries appear advantageous".

INDEX

INDEX

For Product Safety Concerns and Information please contact our EU
representative GPSR@taylorandfrancis.com Taylor & Francis Verlag GmbH,
Kaufingerstraße 24, 80331 München, Germany

Printed and bound by CPI Group (UK) Ltd, Croydon, CR0 4YY
08/05/2025
01864516-0001